# HORRIBLE SCIENCE

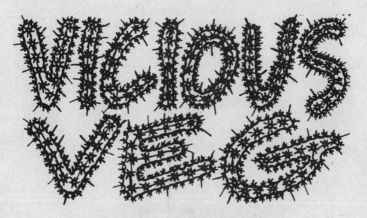

# VICIOUS VEG

## NICK ARNOLD

D1052397

Illustrated by
Tony De Saulles

Hippo

Scholastic Children's Books,
Euston House, 24 Eversholt Street,
London, NW1 1DB, UK
A division of Scholastic Ltd
London ~ New York ~ Toronto ~ Sydney ~ Auckland
Mexico City ~ New Delhi ~ Hong Kong

First published in the UK by Scholastic Ltd, 1998

10 digit ISBN 0 590 19811 4
13 digit ISBN 978 0590 19811 0

Typeset by Rapid Reprographics Ltd, London
Printed and bound in Denmark by Nørhaven Paperback A/S, Viborg

19 20

# Contents

...AND HOW LONG HAS THIS APPLE PIP BEEN STUCK BETWEEN YOUR TEETH, MR SMITH?

**Nick Arnold** has been writing stories and books since he was a youngster, but never dreamt he'd find fame writing about Vicious Veg. His research involved swinging from vines, grappling with strangling plants and dancing in fairy rings and he enjoyed every minute of it.

When he's not delving into Horrible Science, he spends his spare time teaching adults in a college. His hobbies include eating pizza, riding his bike and thinking up corny jokes (though not all at the same time).

**Tony De Saulles** picked up his crayons when he was still in nappies and has been doodling ever since. He takes Horrible Science very seriously and even agreed to sketch foul-smelling plants that ponged of rotting flesh. Fortunately, he has made a full recovery.

When he's not out with his sketchpad, Tony likes to write poetry and play squash, though he hasn't written any poetry about squash yet.

# Introduction

Some science books tell you about plants. You can learn nice little facts about leaves, seeds, fruits and pretty little flowers. But this book is different. It's about plants all right, but it's also about Horrible Science!

So if your science lessons are like this...

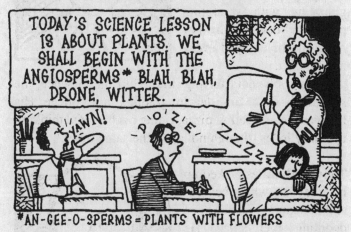

TODAY'S SCIENCE LESSON IS ABOUT PLANTS. WE SHALL BEGIN WITH THE ANGIOSPERMS* BLAH, BLAH, DRONE, WITTER. . .

YAWN!

DOZE ZZZ

*AN-GEE-O-SPERMS = PLANTS WITH FLOWERS

And the only excitement is when someone actually drops off to sleep and your teacher turns vicious...

HUH?

WAKE UP MISS PERKINS, YOU TURNIP-BRAIN!

Maybe you need a helping of Horrible Science. Then you can ask your teacher a few vicious questions...

Now, doesn't that sound a bit more interesting? *Horribly* interesting? And guess what? It's all TRUE. With facts like these at your fingertips you'll be able to show your friends you're a budding scientist, and turn your teacher green with envy.

So there you are. There really is a lot more to plants than silly seeds, fancy flowers and limp leaves. Plants have loads more vicious secrets and many VILE, VILLAINOUS, VIOLENT and VICIOUS tricks. And by some spooky coincidence that's what this book is about – VICIOUS VEG (that's vegetables to you – it's another word for plants). So what are you waiting for? Why not "leaf" through a few pages? You might even find that plant science starts to grow on you...

Welcome to another world. This is a green and terrifying world where horrible things happen every day. A world where death is an ugly tendril slowly reaching out to strangle its victim. A world where there are no rules and the only aim is to stay alive. Welcome to the vicious world of veg.

Unlike animals, plants can't run away, and they can't hide from danger. And danger is everywhere. Take a look at this peaceful country scene. Looks quiet, doesn't it? Maybe a little boring?

Well, you couldn't be more wrong. Now take a closer look. Bigger plants are stealing light from smaller plants…

Trees are stealing light from everyone…

Plant roots are fighting for moisture…

There are millions of guzzling bugs...

Imagine seeing a whole day in a speeded-up film. You'd see the leaves of plants twisting and turning as they follow the sun as it moves across the sky. You'd see plants slowly strangling one another and trying to poison visiting bugs. Like I said, plants are vicious, and we know all about this vicious world thanks to plant scientists. Here's the first of them – a curious Greek named Theophrastus.

### Hall of Fame: Theophrastus (371-287 BC)
Nationality: Greek

Theo is famous because he was the first botanist – that's a person who studies plants. Other people either ate them or grew them, but Theo preferred to study plants very closely and he went on to describe them in a very organized way.

Nothing is known of Theo's early days but he seems to have spent his life working as a teacher in Athens. He was a pal of brainy philosophers such as Plato and Aristotle and he wrote about 200 books in his own write, I mean right. Including a book on plants. In it Theo described over 500 plants such as bananas and flowers from as far afield as India.

He really did a good job of describing them but he also believed a few tall tales. For example, he reckoned a scorpion could be killed by being stroked with a wolfsbane plant and then brought back to life with a touch of the white hellebore plant.

And talking about far-fetched fantasies – it's said Theo lived far longer than the dates given here. It's said he finally threw in his gardening gloves at the ripe old age of 107. Who says greens aren't good for you?

### Could you be a botanist?

So you want to be a botanist? Well, beware. Being a botanist isn't about tiptoeing through the tulips and talking to the trees. Botany is a tough outdoor science. It's more likely to involve exploring horrible places such as stinking swamps in search of rare and vicious plants. And sinking up to your neck in mud that reeks of rotten eggs, and being eaten alive by blood-sucking bugs.

But that's only the start of the horrible things that can happen to botanists. In the nineteenth century botanists travelled all over the world collecting plants and seeds for scientific study, and they faced all kinds of terrible dangers...

# THE ORINOCO NEWS

## *The voice of South America* 1801

## MYSTERY BUG ATE OUR COLLECTION

News just in from botanists Alexandra von Humboldt and Aimé Bonpland somewhere on the Orinoco river. These two brave botanists claim that vicious bugs unknown to science have scoffed most of  their plant collection. Said Humboldt, "We found thousands of brand new plants. Unfortunately, the bugs discovered the plants too." In a bid to make the bugs back off the botanists smeared themselves in alligator fat. Sounds a fat lot of good for our battling botanists.

# THE HAWAII HERALD
## —1834—

# DARING DOUGLAS DEAD!

**P**lant hunter David Douglas is dead. Reports say he fell into a pit trap containing a wild bull while he was looking for rare plant specimens. A police spokesperson said, "The bull was pretty wild at being in the trap."

Douglas, 36, shot to fame when he found thousands of previously unknown plants in North America. These included the Douglas fir - now named after him. Daring Douglas had travelled thousands of miles and had an earlier brush with death when his canoe capsized and he nearly drowned. Here was one botanist who wasn't scared to walk on the wild side.

# THE ARIZONA GAZETTE

1998

# CROOKED CACTUS COWBOYS CAUGHT

The sheriff's office today reports that three cactus rustlers have been rounded up following a tip-off from a botanist. The rustlers, who were armed and dangerous, were taking cacti from the desert without a permit. Stolen cacti fetch huge prices from collectors in Europe and Japan but the ruthless rustlers are wiping these prickly plants out. They take huge numbers and cacti are getting scarce. And because these giant greens are so slow growing it will take ages before new cacti can grow and take their place. A botanist in the State Conservation Department said, "Cacti rustling sure is a prickly problem."

## Vicious plant types

So you know the dangers and you're still keen to be a botanist? Well, you're going to need a bit of vital info to get you started. We'll start off with the basics. So you reckon you'd know a plant if you bumped into one? Well, now you can cultivate your knowledge a bit more…

### Vicious veg fact file

**NAME:** Plants

**THE BASIC FACTS:** According to scientists, a plant is a living thing that makes its food from sunlight. Its leaves are usually green. If you break a plant's leaves colour rubs off on your hands. That's why some people say gardeners have green fingers. Ha ha!

**THE VICIOUS DETAILS:**

**1** Some plants spice up their diet with dead insects. They catch the insects and then dissolve their bodies or suck out their insides (see page 57 for the details).

**2** Some plants happily feed on blood through their roots. (Dried blood is used in some fertilizers. It contains vital chemicals known as minerals that plants need.)

WOW! THAT PLANT'S GROWN QUICKLY!

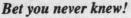

*Bet you never knew!*

*Blood is only one ingredient of some traditional fertilizers. Here's a genuine revolting recipe...*

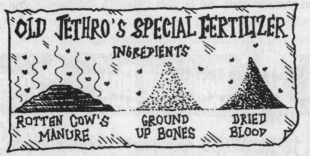

OLD JETHRO'S SPECIAL FERTILIZER

INGREDIENTS

ROTTEN COW'S MANURE

GROUND UP BONES

DRIED BLOOD

*These revolting ingredients are rich in minerals. The plants can take the chemicals in through their roots and use them to grow and stay healthy.*

## Could you be a botanist?

OK, now for the next stage in your training. There's something else you need to know before you can get stuck into that swamp.

## What plants are made of

Look closely at a plant and you'll see it's made up of cells. These minute jelly-like objects make up all plants and animals. The sides of plant cells are strengthened with a substance called cellulose (cell-u-loze).

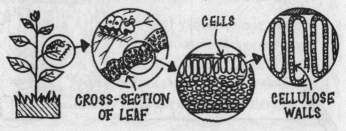

CELLS

CROSS-SECTION OF LEAF

CELLULOSE WALLS

Cellulose is the stuff that makes greens stringy. It makes up the roughage in your diet which helps your body move your half-digested food through your guts. Most cellulose ends up in your poo. (Just in case you were wondering.)

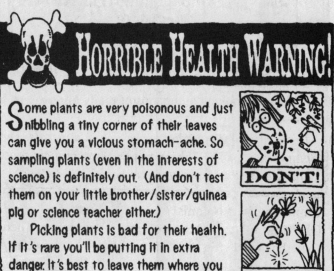

# HORRIBLE HEALTH WARNING!

Some plants are very poisonous and just nibbling a tiny corner of their leaves can give you a vicious stomach-ache. So sampling plants (even in the interests of science) is definitely out. (And don't test them on your little brother/sister/guinea pig or science teacher either.)

**DON'T!**

Picking plants is bad for their health. If it's rare you'll be putting it in extra danger. It's best to leave them where you find them.

**DON'T!**

## Have you got the vital equipment?

Magnifying glass for looking at really small plants such as this duckweed.

WOW! THAT'S SMALL!

0·3mm

DUCKWEED

DUCK WEE!

Microscope for looking really closely at plants and for checking out even tinier plants such as algae.

MICROSCOPE GLASS SLIDE

STRAY TADPOLE

Binoculars for looking at the tops of really big trees such as this sequoia.

GIANT SEQUOIA TREES IN CALIFORNIA*

MIAOW!

DON'T JUMP, PUSS!

*These beautiful trees are the largest on Earth. One heartless person reckoned that if just one giant sequoia was cut down it could make five billion matchsticks.

NOTEBOOK, PEN AND CAMERA TO RECORD PLANTS WITHOUT PICKING THEM

VEGETATION OBSERVED ON EXPEDITION

VEGETATION EATEN ON EXPEDITION

Got all that? Now you're almost ready to start your career as a botanist! Here's a handy identification guide to help you spot the main groups of plants.

**Baffling bacteria** (Number of species [individual types] is unknown. It's thought that 90 per cent of them are still unknown to science.)

Chances are you've got a few million of these crawling on you. Don't panic! We all have – 'cos bacteria are everywhere. You'll find them lurking about in the depths of the ocean as well as in the depths of your toilet. Bacteria are tiny blobs of matter so small that millions can fit on the point of a drawing pin (just don't go sitting on the drawing pin). That's because some vicious bacteria cause disease although many others are quite harmless. Some even live in your guts and make vitamins K and B to keep you healthy.

> **IMPORTANT NOTE**
> Bacteria aren't really plants at all – they're not green and they don't have roots or leaves – but they do affect plants. That's why they're in this book.

**Foul fungi** (70,000 species)

Fungi are plants that lack chlorophyll – that's the green stuff most plants use to make food from sunshine. Foul fungi include the mildew in your bathroom, the mushrooms swimming in your soup and the mould on your school dinner. And beware – all fungi guzzle animals or plants – either dead or alive. When they feed, they turn their victim into nourishing soup and slurp up the juices. Tastee! (See page 94 for more details.)

## Awesome algae (25,000 species)

You'll find algae everywhere – from Antarctica to your local pond where they give the water that lovely muddy green colour. The sea in particular is alive with algae. Some are revolting tiny slimy squirming things that are smaller than a pinhead and others are enormous, like the giant seaweeds 60 metres (200 feet) long found off the coast of California, Japan and New Zealand. Yes, that's right, seaweeds are algae too.

*Bet you never knew!*
*Algae can poison the sea. Algae guzzle the chemicals found in the sewage that humans dump in the sea. Well, there's no accounting for taste, is there? Sometimes algae multiply uncontrollably and form huge blooms of vicious algae that use up the oxygen from the water and suffocate fish. (Oxygen, by the way, is the gas that humans and animals need to breathe to stay alive.) Some algae make chemicals that can poison humans swimming in the water, or dogs drinking it. The only things that aren't killed are certain kinds of bacteria. But they make horrible rotten egg smells. Fancy a dip?*

## Loathsome lichens (20,000 species)

A lichen isn't a single plant at all. It's a sort of double act with algae and fungi living together so closely that they seem to be the same plant. The fungi are good at sucking up water, dissolving rock and getting at minerals. The algae can make sunlight into food. It all sounds very cosy. So why are lichens loathsome? Well, it's just an opinion really. Swedish scientist Carl Linnaeus (1707-

1778) made up the system of Latin names for plants that is still used. But Carl didn't like lichens for some reason. He called them: "... the poorest vegetable rubbish."

**Drippy liverworts and mosses** (20,000 species)
These are actually different types of plants but they enjoy (if enjoy is the right word) a similar lifestyle. Basically this involves sitting around in a damp shady spot and staying as wet as possible. Sounds like fun – I don't think. But they have a rather unusual life story...

• The adult plant makes lots of tiny spores (what they have instead of seeds).
• These DON'T develop into adult plants. Instead they form small leaf-like objects.
• These tiny plants make special male and female cells that join together.
• They grow into a new adult plant.

Sounds a load of bother. Botanists call this "alternation of generations" – which means big plants making little plants making big plants and so on. If this happened to humans your parents would be 1 cm long (0.4 inches) and you'd be normal size. But at least there wouldn't be any arguments over pocket money!

## Gigantic gymnosperms (700 species)

Gymnosperm (Jim-no-spurm) means "naked seed" in Greek. This simply means that seeds on these plants are open to the air rather than wrapped up in a flower.

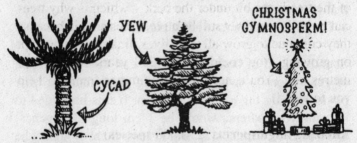

Well-known gymnosperms include all pine trees, yew trees and a rather ancient species of plants called a cycad that was once munched by dinosaurs. Those cycads must be the oldest salads in the world – yes, even older than that limp lettuce you get with your school dinner.

### Trees

Trees aren't a proper group of plants. A tree is just a giant plant with a woody stem to hold it up. (We can't have trees flopping over, can we?) The woody stuff is a substance called lignin that's dumped in the centre of the tree.

PERHAPS IT'S A RUBBER TREE

This means at school you probably sit on a lump of lignin. And in days gone by your vicious teacher might have whacked you with a length of lignin. The living part of the tree is the bit under the bark – which is why trees can be hollow and yet still be alive. Trees are big because they continue to grow all their lives. Imagine if you kept on growing. You could end up 300 years old and 100 metres tall. (You'd need a *giant* zimmer frame to help you to walk!)

**Amazing angiosperms** (250,000 species)
These are flowering plants, remember? They are a huge plant group that includes just about everything that people might grow in their gardens. And just about everything that would ever turn up in a school dinner salad (excluding the odd caterpillar).

Flowering plants produce flowers (howls of amazement) as a way of spreading their pollen to other flowers of the same species. After they've received the pollen some parts of the flowers turn into fruits and seeds (see page 107 for the amazing details). Then we humans or just about any other hungry creature get to munch them. Mind you, the plant gets the last laugh. More often than not the seeds pass through the animal's guts and reappear later with a nice dollop of dung to help them grow.

So as you can see, plants come in all shapes and sizes. Some look fairly ordinary but they're all really gobsmacking. I mean just read on and you'll see why…

Some people think plants are boring. But they couldn't be more wrong. And here's the most amazing fact of all. Plants are the *main* form of life on Earth. In fact, the Earth ought to be renamed Planet Plant. (Planet Vegetable or Planet Turnip would sound a bit too ridiculous!)

**Planetary plant facts**

Imagine you're an alien looking at Earth from your spacecraft. At first, you might think that plants actually ruled the Earth. I mean, take a good look. Spot any humans? Nope – they're too small. But you can see plants, can't you? Loads of them.

See that huge smudge of green on the northern part of the world? That's millions and millions of trees that make up the vast pine forests that stretch across Asia from Norway to Canada. And those greeny blobs in South America, Africa and South-east Asia? They're rainforests. OK, there are fewer forests since humans started cutting them down for roads and farms. But you get the idea.

So the Earth is absolutely teeming with plants. If you weighed every living object on Earth you'd find that 99.9 per cent of this massive weight is plants. And only 0.1 per cent is made up of animals (and that includes big heavy animals like overweight elephants).

OK, so if plants are so amazingly widespread that means teachers must know loads of gobsmacking plant facts. Right? Here's your chance to find out. Does your teacher have green fingers? Or is their knowledge rather weedy?

**Test your teacher**
Even a chimp can get one third of these questions right 'cos there are only three possible answers. So how will your teacher get on?
**1** How much ground can one grass plant cover?
**a)** One square metre (1.2 square yards)
**b)** As much as a small garden.
**c)** As much as a large field.

**2** How long can a seed survive before it dies?
**a)** Ten months
**b)** Ten years
**c)** Ten thousand years

**3** Some types of plants puff out gas from their leaves. This is taken in through the leaves of another plant of the same species (type of plant). The gas carries a message but what is it?
**a)** I lurve your flowers.
**b)** Make more fruit.
**c)** BEWARE – hungry giraffes on the rampage.

26

**4** Where WON'T you find a plant growing?
**a)** Between your toes.
**b)** Inside a solid rock.
**c)** Underneath the snow in the Antarctic.

**5** What do some plants do if you breathe on them?
**a)** Turn your breath to a poisonous gas and puff it back at you.
**b)** Wilt
**c)** Turn your breath into sugar and eat it.

**6** What substance is NEVER made by trees?
**a)** A red fluid that looks suspiciously like blood.
**b)** Dew
**c)** The stuff they use to make chocolate.

**7** How do some plants keep warm?
**a)** Central heating
**b)** Hairy leaves
**c)** By shivering

**8** What do some plants do when they're thirsty?
**a)** Grow special windows in their leaves that let the sun in without letting water out.
**b)** Cut bits off their own bodies.
**c)** Cover themselves in a sort of cling-film.

**9** Which of these objects is NOT a plant?
**a)** A bird's dropping
**b)** A weird mushroom-shaped object
**c)** A pebble

**Answers:**

**1 c)** A single plant can really grow this big. Scientists have found that a field of fescue (that's a type of grass) is often a single plant. This can be hundreds of years old and still growing strong.

**2 c)** Amazing but true. In 1982 Japanese scientists found a ten-thousand-year-old magnolia seed in an old storage pit. They planted it and the incredible seed sprouted into a healthy plant.

**3 c)** Yes – acacia trees say it with flowers. Or more accurately with their leaves. When an African acacia is attacked by a hungry giraffe its leaves make a foul-tasting poison to put the giraffe off. They also puff out ethylene (eth-ey-lene) gas. Nearby acacia trees take in the gas through tiny holes in their leaves called stomata (sto-mart-a) and start making the poison as well.

**4** Trick question! Plants grow in *all* of these places. **a)** If your toes are dirty enough you might find *anything* there – especially fungi. Even the cheesy pong doesn't kill them off. Check out the vicious details on page 97.

**b)** Some algae in Antarctica live inside sandstone rock. The algae get in through cracks in the rock. They're kept alive by sunlight that filters through see-through grains in the rock.

**c)** Other Antarctic algae live in snow. They swim around in the snow using special swimming hairs and make a kind of anti-freeze to stop their bodies from freezing up. They'd be quite at home in your favourite ice-cream.

**5 c)** Your breath contains carbon dioxide gas. A plant takes this in through tiny holes in their leaves called stomata and turns the carbon into sugar. The plant uses the sugar as energy to grow. It might send some to its flowers to make nectar. If a bee makes the nectar into honey you might end up eating the carbon from your own breath. Hmm.

**6 b)** Although you might find drops of dew on trees the dew is actually tiny drops of water that form in the air. So dew is not made by plants.

**a)** The red stuff is a kind of gum that oozes from the Australian bloodwood tree if you cut its bark. The gum protects the cut as it heals, and you can guess how it got its name. Yep, it's ideal for vegetarian vampires. Aborigines use the juice to heal wounds and as a gargle for sore throats.

AND I MEET A LOT OF PEOPLE WITH SORE THROATS

**c)** Chocolate is made from the crushed seeds of the cacao tree.

**7 b)** Edelweiss plants have hairy leaves to keep them warm in the cold air of the Alps where they grow. Lobelia flowers on Mount Kenya in East Africa grow on a hairy stem. The hair protects the flowers from freezing just like a little fur coat.

COPY CAT!

**8** Trick question. Plants do *all* these things. Give your teacher ONE mark for saying "all of them". But a miserable half a mark for suggesting either **a)**, **b)** or **c)**.

**a)** Window plants in the Namib desert in south-west Africa make special see-through crystals to protect their leaves from the hot sun. It's a bit like wearing sun cream.

**b)** Plants lose water through their stomata. The Namibian quiver tree grows a wall inside its trunk to cut off a branch. The branch has to fall off. That means there are fewer leaves to lose water.

**c)** Many plants protect themselves from drying out by pumping out a waxy layer from their stomata. This covers the leaves and stops them from losing water.

**9** Ha ha – another nasty trick question. They're *all* plants.

**a)** is an anacampseros (anna-camp-ser-ros) plant that lives in dry areas. It looks like a bird dropping in order to deter animals from eating it. Fancy one in your salad?

**b)** is a stromatolite (stro-mat-o-lite) – that's a weird blob of algae and mud that's found on some Australian beaches. It's sculpted into a mushroom shape by the sea.

**c)** is a pebble plant from the deserts of Africa. It disguises itself to look like a pebble to stop animals eating it. Well, stone me.

## What your teacher's score means:

**9** Impossible. NO teacher in history has ever scored this high … unless they've been secretly peeking at this book. If so, confiscate the book *at once*. You can't have your teacher knowing more than you, can you?

**7-8** BEWARE. Your teacher is a secret botanist. Signs to look for are green fingers, dirt under the fingernails, half-crazed expression, always talking about plants, knowing all the Latin names of plants, etc.

**4-6** Average – could try harder. Just a common or garden teacher, really.

**0-3** This is sad. Your teacher obviously needs to turn over a new leaf and do some extra botany homework.

One of the most gobsmacking things about plants is the way they eat. And do plants like to eat! They feed themselves all day long … just like some humans, really. But their eating habits can be very different. Read on for the vicious details.

YUMMY!

MENU
CARBON DIOXIDE
SUNLIGHT
WATER

# GREEDY GREENERY

Imagine you had ultra-powerful hearing. If you went outside you'd be able to hear a quiet slurping noise that would be the sound of thousands of plants busily guzzling their food.

But plants don't eat stuff like cream cakes. Oh no – a plant can make a meal of just three simple ingredients. Water, air and sunshine.

OK, so you don't believe me? Well, read on and find out for yourself...

**Vicious veg expressions**

Doesn't she need a camera?

Can you imagine what it would be like if all you had to do when you wanted to eat was to lie about in the sun. Life would be brilliant, wouldn't it? Then, when you woke up your food would be ready for you. This incredible process was discovered by a desperately shy scientist who managed to needle just about everyone.

## Hall of fame: Jan Ingen-Housz (1730-1799)
Nationality: Dutch

You could tell young Jan was going to do something brainy when he grew up, he was that kind of kid. Clever. But no one guessed he was going to be a scientist. Young Jan himself wanted to be a doctor. He studied at universities in Belgium and Holland and sure enough he went on to be a successful doctor.

He went to England in 1764 and heard about the new-fangled science called inoculation. This was a way of stopping people from getting the killer disease smallpox. Doctors pricked them with a needle and thread that were coated with smallpox germs taken from the gory pus of a sick person. The idea was that by giving a few germs to a healthy body the body would learn how to protect itself from the killer disease. But the operation was risky – it sometimes went horribly wrong. The needle might carry too many germs and cause the patient to develop full-blown smallpox and die.

Well, Jan got busy with his needle and in a few months he had inoculated over 700 people. The British king, George III (1738-1820) was so impressed he sent Jan to Austria with instructions to inoculate the Austrian royal family. It was a horribly dangerous job for Jan. If he got it wrong he might kill the Empress of Austria with his needle!

SORRY, I'M HAVING T-T-TROUBLE THREADING THE N-N-N-NEEDLE

But the operation was a success. The Empress stayed healthy and she never caught smallpox. As a result Jan was given loads of expensive presents.

In the 1770s, during a stay in England, Jan became interested in the gases plants made. This had nothing to do with inoculation and it all came about because Jan read about the work of scientist Joseph Priestly (1733-1804), who found out that plants seemed to make and soak up mysterious gases. So Jan decided to do some experiments of his own.

He eventually proved that plants take in the gas we now call carbon dioxide and spray out oxygen. He then went on to prove that this only happened in green parts of the plant that were exposed to light. BINGO! Jan had discovered photosynthesis. He later proved that plant cells also take in oxygen and give out carbon dioxide. So plants also "breathe" just like us.

Jan was interested in lots of other areas of science and he went on to design a machine (which he never got round to building) to help patients with breathing problems by giving them pure oxygen.

## Precious plants

Now here's the really BIG news. Without photosynthesis we'd all be as dead as an oven-ready dodo.

1 Plants make oxygen by photosynthesis and we breathe it in. And 70 per cent of the Earth's oxygen comes from

the sea. This vital gas is made by trillions of algae that float around in the waves. So it's basically plants that keep us humans alive.

**2** No animal can do without oxygen for more than a few minutes. And if you added up all the oxygen used by all the animals on Earth in just one second it would come to 10,000 tons (10,160 tonnes). That's an awful lot of puffing and panting.

**3** Scientists reckon there's enough oxygen around to last us about 3,000 years. After that, without plants to make more oxygen we'll all be gasping. Now 3,000 years might sound like a really long time. But it's nothing compared to the three billion years that plants have been around on Earth.

And plants are vital for other reasons too.

**4** Just imagine getting up in the morning. Horrible thought, isn't it? But it would be far tougher if you didn't have any energy at all. The energy that gets you up came from the food energy in that lovely burger and fries that you had for supper.

**5** And all of that came from plants. Plants? Well, yes…

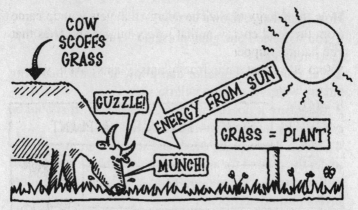

COW SCOFFS GRASS

GUZZLE!

ENERGY FROM SUN

GRASS = PLANT

MUNCH!

Some grass ends up in a smelly cow pat. But its energy doesn't go to waste.

POO – WASTE GRASS

POOH!

PLOP!

Poo rots into soil and is eaten up by greedy fungi and grass. And so all the food in plants (and the cow and the fungi) was originally built up using photosynthesis.

*Bet you never knew!*
*The power to cook your supper in a microwave or electric cooker comes from electricity. This may have come from burning coal at a power station. And guess what? Coal also comes from plants. Yes, coal is made from ancient plants (a few species of which are still knocking around) called clubmosses and horsetails.*

How to make your own coal…

**1** You will need one giant horsetail – say 40 metres (140 feet) in height.

**2** Cut down the horsetail and allow it to rot in warm, smelly water. A swamp will do.

**3** Make sure it doesn't rot away completely. It should be covered by layers of more half-rotted horsetails.

**4** Squash down really hard, and leave to simmer gently under the ground for a good length of time, say about 350 million years. Oh, and don't forget to keep adding more layers of mud and sand.

**5** Remove from the ground and burn.

You should find that with all this squashing your horsetail has turned into hard, black coal. But coal is simply carbon from the carbon dioxide taken in by the horsetail by photosynthesis all those years ago. Worth the wait wasn't it?

## Powerful plant plans

Let's take a closer look at a typical plant:

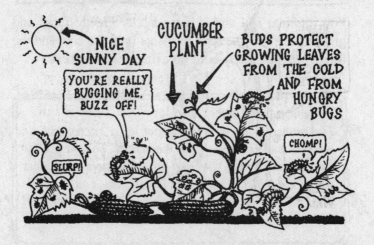

# A close up view of a leaf

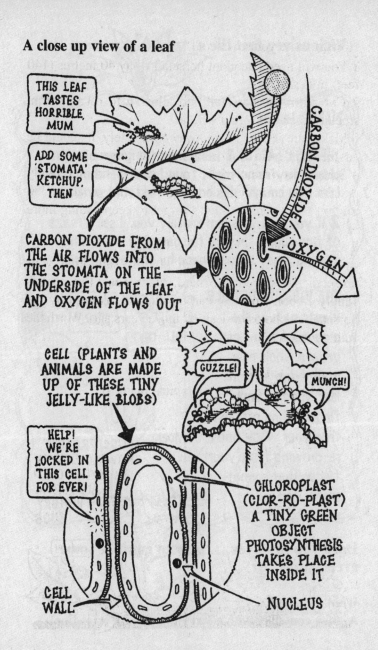

THIS LEAF TASTES HORRIBLE, MUM

ADD SOME 'STOMATA' KETCHUP, THEN

CARBON DIOXIDE

OXYGEN

CARBON DIOXIDE FROM THE AIR FLOWS INTO THE STOMATA ON THE UNDERSIDE OF THE LEAF AND OXYGEN FLOWS OUT

CELL (PLANTS AND ANIMALS ARE MADE UP OF THESE TINY JELLY-LIKE BLOBS)

GUZZLE!

MUNCH!

HELP! WE'RE LOCKED IN THIS CELL FOR EVER!

CHLOROPLAST (CLOR-RO-PLAST) A TINY GREEN OBJECT PHOTOSYNTHESIS TAKES PLACE INSIDE IT

CELL WALL

NUCLEUS

# Vicious veg fact file

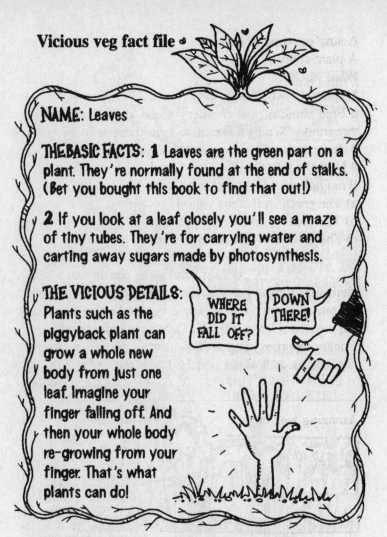

**NAME**: Leaves

**THE BASIC FACTS**: **1** Leaves are the green part on a plant. They're normally found at the end of stalks. (Bet you bought this book to find that out!)

**2** If you look at a leaf closely you'll see a maze of tiny tubes. They're for carrying water and carting away sugars made by photosynthesis.

**THE VICIOUS DETAILS**: Plants such as the piggyback plant can grow a whole new body from just one leaf. Imagine your finger falling off. And then your whole body re-growing from your finger. That's what plants can do!

WHERE DID IT FALL OFF?

DOWN THERE!

**Dare you discover ... how to capture some green slime?**

*What you need:*
A glass container with a screw top (a jam jar is fine)

A strip of wood or bark

A plant spray

*What you do:*

1 Spray the wood with water.

2 Find some of that powdery green algae that lives on tree trunks. Scrape some on to your damp strip of wood.

3 Place the wood in the jar and seal the lid.

4 Leave in a light place for a few days.

*What happens next?*

**a)** The green stuff turns yellow.

**b)** The green stuff starts to spread.

**c)** The green stuff glows in the dark.

---

**Answer:**

**b)** The algae are using carbon dioxide from the air, sunshine and the water you gave them to make sugars. This gives them the energy to grow. If a), it needs a bit more light and possibly water. If c), you have found an alien life form. Beware, because it might start squishing out of the jar and frightening the cat.

---

## Amazing leaf facts

There's nothing thrilling about this leaf? Well, get your teeth into these fantastic facts...

1 The leaves of the sensitive plant are surprisingly... sensitive. If you touch them the stem bows down to the ground and the plant folds into a spike. This puts off most

hungry animals – well, it would, wouldn't it? Have you ever had a salad that tried to escape?

**2** What happens is that the touch triggers an electrical current inside the leaf. This empties all the liquid out of cells in the base of the leaves and makes them collapse. So remember this plant is sensitive and don't go upsetting it by saying cruel things like "vinaigrette dressing".

**3** Some of the biggest leaves belong to a species of arum plant. Its huge leaves are three metres (ten feet) wide. Some travellers use them as tents but you can also eat them. (Note: It's a bad idea to nibble holes in your tent.)

**4** Talking about huge leaves – Amazon water lily leaves are two metres (6.6 feet) across. They're so strong that the first gardener to grow them, Joseph Paxton (1801-1865), dressed his daughter as a fairy and photographed her sitting on a leaf. Bet she felt a right idiot. (This won't work with normal-sized water lilies.)

CHILD SITTING ON GIANT AMAZON WATER LILY

CHILD SITTING ON NORMAL WATER LILY

**5** Ever wondered why leaves turn pretty colours and fall in autumn? Well, amazingly, the leaves are pushed out by the tree! In cold countries it's tough for trees in the winter. They find it hard to suck up water from the cold soil. It's a bit like you trying to suck ice-cream through a straw. So the trees shut up shop. There's no use keeping those useless water-losing leaves.

**6** Those pretty colours come from leftover and unwanted chemicals in the leaves. The valuable green colour from the chloroplasts gets sucked back into the tree whilst more waste chemicals pour into the leaf.

**7** And when the leaf falls it's like the tree is going to the toilet – or should that be lav-a-tree? The tree makes chemicals that loosen the stalk from the branch. So it flutters gently down to earth. And by some revolting coincidence that's exactly where we're heading.

To understand plants you need to go back to your roots. That's to say, take a look below the surface of plants and see what's going on in the cold dark soil, and probe its revolting secrets. Hope you've got a really strong stomach.

## Revolting down-to-earth details

Try to imagine soil as an entire world – a secret underground city full of tiny rooms. That's what you see through a microscope. Each tiny grain of soil is surrounded by stuff called humus, rather like a chocolate-coated nut (no, don't try to eat soil – it tastes disgusting – read on to find out why).

Humus is made up of tiny rotting lumps of plants and animals and poo all mixed together. Oh, and not forgetting bacteria – billions and trillions of bacteria. A large pinch of soil – just four cubic centimetres (one quarter of a square inch) – holds five billion bacteria. That's almost as many bacteria as there are humans on Earth.

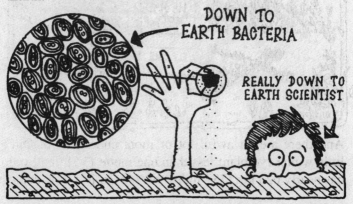

DOWN TO
EARTH BACTERIA

REALLY DOWN TO
EARTH SCIENTIST

If these bacteria were the size of a person, that pinch of soil would be the height of a skyscraper 10,000 floors high. If you spread all the muck you'll find in just 28 grams (one ounce) of fine soil it would make a thin layer covering four hectares (ten acres) – that's the size of a small city. And all this slime binds the tiny grains of soil together and stops them from blowing away.

It sounds gross but this secret unseen world is a happy hunting ground for millions of tiny bugs called mites. And there are also larger bugs and squirming worms as well as fungi all happily hunting and scrunching one another. Then there are plant roots blindly searching for minerals and water in the soil. (Minerals are chemicals that plants need to grow and stay strong and healthy, remember? They include potassium, phosphorus and nitrates.)

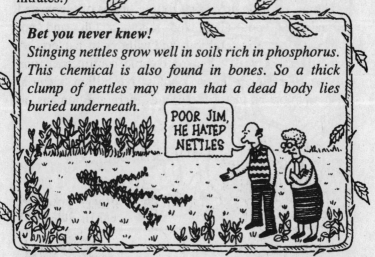

**Bet you never knew!**
*Stinging nettles grow well in soils rich in phosphorus. This chemical is also found in bones. So a thick clump of nettles may mean that a dead body lies buried underneath.*

POOR JIM, HE HATED NETTLES

And there are an awful lot of roots underground. One little winter rye plant less than one metre (3.28 feet) tall has nearly 623 km (387 miles) of roots in just 0.06 cubic

**47**

metres (two cubic feet) of soil. In fact, if you stretched out all the plant roots in just one average-sized garden they'd stretch all the way round the moon *and* back again.

## The root of the problem

If it wasn't for their roots plants would really be falling down on the job. Let's take a slightly different look at that cucumber plant...

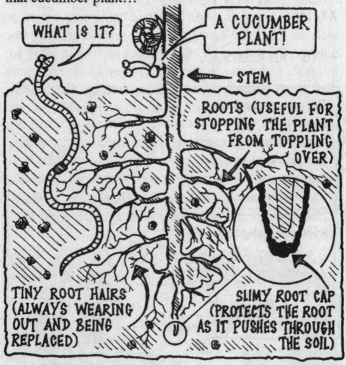

The root hairs suck up water and minerals. These are sucked up to the leaves though tubes called xylem (zy-lem). Sugar made by photosynthesis moves around in other tubes called phloem (flow-em).

And here's an X-ray view of the cucumber plant's stem.

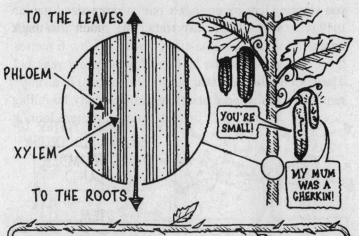

TO THE LEAVES

PHLOEM

XYLEM

TO THE ROOTS

YOU'RE SMALL!

MY MUM WAS A GHERKIN!

*Bet you never knew!*
Some plant roots actually improve the soil. Roots of plants called legumes (related to peas), contain bacteria that turn nitrogen gas from the air in the soil into nitrate chemicals that other plants use once the legume has died.

**Vicious veg expressions**

IT'S TRANSPIRATION!

Shouldn't that be perspiration?

No, she's talking about her plant. Transpiration is when plants soak up water through their roots and lose it through the stomata in their leaves. This ensures a stream

49

of water to their leaves for photosynthesis. It's a bit like you slurping a drink through a really long straw.

Plants lose huge amounts of water through transpiration. An average-sized lawn – 15.2 x 6 metres (50 x 20 feet) – can lose 50 tons of water every year and a large tree can lose 1,000 litres (220 gallons) in a single sunny day. No wonder plants get thirsty.

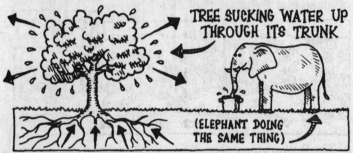

TREE SUCKING WATER UP THROUGH ITS TRUNK

(ELEPHANT DOING THE SAME THING)

## Dare you discover … transpiration?

*What you need:*
A plant
A polythene bag
An elastic band

*What you do is:*
**1** Cover a branch and a few leaves with the polythene bag.
**2** Secure the edges of the bag with the elastic band so that air can't get into the bag.
**3** Leave it in a sunny place for four hours.
*What do you notice?*
**a)** The bag has been sucked in.
**b)** The bag has been blown outwards.
**c)** The inside of the bag is covered with tiny water droplets.

**Could you be a botanist?**

**1** You're looking for plants near the Arctic Circle and you
find some pretty flowers growing in the decaying skeleton
of an animal. Why are they there?

**a)** The flowers were there first and the animal died on top
of them.

**b)** The flowers were poisonous. The animal ate the
flowers and died.

**c)** The animal died first. The flowers sprouted later and
fed on the nourishing rotting bones.

**2** You find these roots growing on a seashore. Why are
they sticking upwards? (Roots normally grow sideways
or downwards.)

**a)** To breathe air.

**b)** To stab passing animals and suck their blood.

c) To stop mud being washed away by the sea and so build up some nice solid soil for the plant to grow on.

**Answers:**

**1 c)** The soil is very poor but the rain has washed nourishing minerals from the dead body into the soil. So the flowers flourish. The skeleton also protects the plants from the biting wind.

**2 a)** They're a type of mangrove root. They stick out of the water to take in air. When the tide comes in they stop taking in air and the plant has to hold its breath until the tide goes out.

Mind you, the next chapter might leave you bit breathless. The plants you're about to meet are extra *vicious*. They are quite capable of using fiendish traps and tricks to capture bugs and small animals and then ... dinner time!

DON'T LET THEM GET US!

# Vicious bug-eating Veg

*CHOMP!* *GUZZLE!* *SLURP!*

Plants sit around doing nothing. Animals eat the plants. It's the law of nature. Well, not necessarily. Some plants bite back ... and they eat animals. Welcome to the nightmare world of bug-eating vegetables...

**Vicious veg fact file**

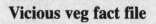

**NAME:** Bug-eating plants

**THE BASIC FACTS:** In some swampy areas there aren't enough minerals to feed plants. The soil is especially low in the nitrates that plants need to grow. Plants help themselves to extra nitrates by scoffing insects.

> HAVE YOU GOT ANTS IN YOUR PANTS?

> NO. I'VE GOT BUGS IN MY PETTICOATS!

**THE VICIOUS DETAILS:** Some bug-eating plants look pretty. The Australian pink petticoat plant looks like a tiny pink petticoat. (How sweet!) But an unwary bug that crawls inside finds itself in a trap and is digested ... alive.

### The lost lunch-break

Imagine a vast table-shaped mountain 2,700 metres (9,000 feet) high. It's so high and so steep that waterfalls cascade down its sides and turn to steam before they hit the ground. The summit of this mountain is lost in dense, gloomy clouds. This is the sinister and mysterious realm of Roraima in South America. What horrible secrets does it hide?

One British botanist was determined to find out. He was brave, or perhaps a bit foolish. His name was Everard Im Thurn (1852-1932). When Everard wasn't busy with his botany, he had a full-time job with the regional government. This is what his diary *might* have looked like (OK – it probably didn't)…

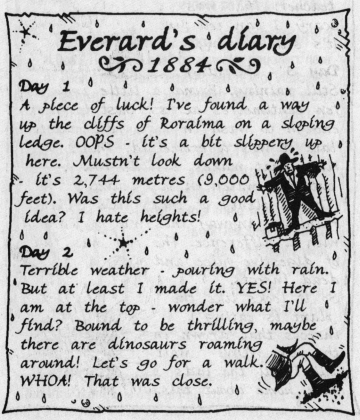

## Everard's diary
### ∽ 1884 ∾

**Day 1**
A piece of luck! I've found a way up the cliffs of Roraima on a sloping ledge. OOPS - it's a bit slippery up here. Mustn't look down - it's 2,744 metres (9,000 feet). Was this such a good idea? I hate heights!

**Day 2**
Terrible weather - pouring with rain. But at least I made it. YES! Here I am at the top - wonder what I'll find? Bound to be thrilling, maybe there are dinosaurs roaming around! Let's go for a walk. WHOA! That was close.

All the rocks up here are covered in slippery, slimy black algae. And there are massive cracks in the rock 30 metres (100 feet) deep. I nearly fell into one. The rocks are awesome. Some look like mushrooms and some like ruined temples. I've even found one that looks like my old science teacher! That was scary, I can tell you! It's still raining.

**Day 3** - Morning
Still raining. Found a little pool a few centimetres across. Just large enough to wash in . . . realized too late it was a bromeliad. That's a plant that makes a little pool by catching water in its leaves. (There's plenty of that - it's STILL raining.) Anyway this was a plant with a difference. The pool was full of digestive juice and dead insects. So it looks like the plant is eating insects that drown in the pool. WOW! - wait till I tell the lads back home about this.

Afternoon - still raining!
Looked more closely at the bromeliad
and found tiny plants and creatures
actually living in the pool. Somehow
they aren't getting digested. The tiny
plants are bladderworts and they're
eating the animals by sucking them
into little pockets in their leaves and
digesting them! A bug-eating plant
inside a bug-eating plant. This place
is seriously weird. IT'S GREAT!
Pity I'm soaked through.

**Day 4**
Still raining - sigh!
Looks like I've accidentally discovered
a new kind of pitcher plant. It works
a bit like the bromeliad I found, by
trapping insects in a pool of
water and leaving them to
rot. Of course the pitcher
plant is a different shape...

  I guess the pitcher plant feeds on
the rotting bodies. Fascinating.

Later. . .
I'm not feeling too good. Don't think
it's the pitcher plant, though. Think
it's all this rain. I'm sure I'm
getting a cold. ATISHOOO!
I feel awful. Time to go home. . .

Bug-eating plants seem horribly mysterious, don't they? I mean – how exactly do they catch their victims? And what do the vicious vegetables do next? Are you brave enough to read all the revolting details? Go on, you know you want to...

## Mysteries of bug-eating plants
### The sundew plant
Found all over the world from Australia to the USA. A sundew plant works like this...

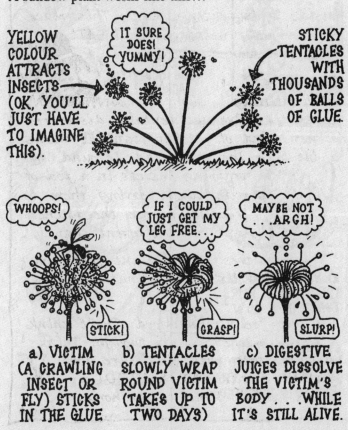

YELLOW COLOUR ATTRACTS INSECTS (OK, YOU'LL JUST HAVE TO IMAGINE THIS).

IT SURE DOES! YUMMY!

STICKY TENTACLES WITH THOUSANDS OF BALLS OF GLUE.

WHOOPS!

IF I COULD JUST GET MY LEG FREE...

MAYBE NOT ...ARGH!

STICK!

GRASP!

SLURP!

a) VICTIM (A CRAWLING INSECT OR FLY) STICKS IN THE GLUE

b) TENTACLES SLOWLY WRAP ROUND VICTIM (TAKES UP TO TWO DAYS)

c) DIGESTIVE JUICES DISSOLVE THE VICTIM'S BODY. . .WHILE IT'S STILL ALIVE.

## The waterwheel plant

Found in Europe, Australia and Africa.

The waterwheel plant lives in ponds and eats tiny pond creatures.

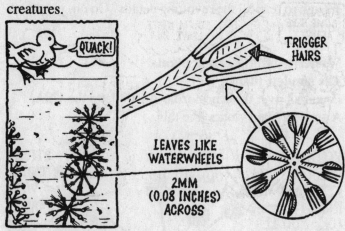

QUACK!

TRIGGER HAIRS

LEAVES LIKE WATERWHEELS

2MM (0.08 INCHES) ACROSS

And here's what happens...

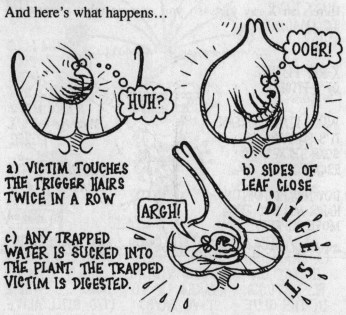

HUH?

OOER!

a) VICTIM TOUCHES THE TRIGGER HAIRS TWICE IN A ROW

b) SIDES OF LEAF CLOSE

ARGH!

c) ANY TRAPPED WATER IS SUCKED INTO THE PLANT. THE TRAPPED VICTIM IS DIGESTED.

DIGEST!

# The pitcher plant
Found in the USA, South America and Australia.

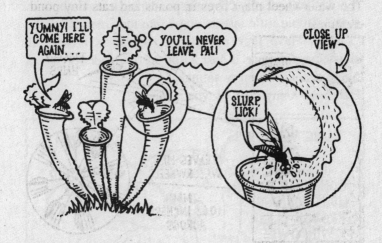

Here's an X-ray view so you can see what's going on inside...

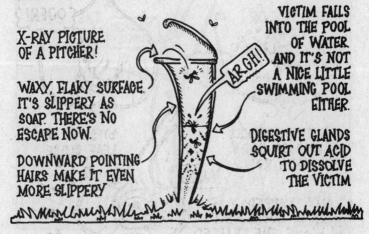

X-RAY PICTURE OF A PITCHER!

WAXY, FLAKY SURFACE. IT'S SLIPPERY AS SOAP. THERE'S NO ESCAPE NOW.

DOWNWARD POINTING HAIRS MAKE IT EVEN MORE SLIPPERY

ARGH!

VICTIM FALLS INTO THE POOL OF WATER AND IT'S NOT A NICE LITTLE SWIMMING POOL EITHER.

DIGESTIVE GLANDS SQUIRT OUT ACID TO DISSOLVE THE VICTIM

## The cobra lily

Found in the USA.

 Looks like a deadly cobra snake rearing up and about to strike. Stupid little insects crawl into the "mouth" of the "snake". Have they no brains? (Scientists reckon its sinister appearance is just a sinister coincidence, not a bid to scare off hungry animals.)

Here's an X-ray view of what happens...

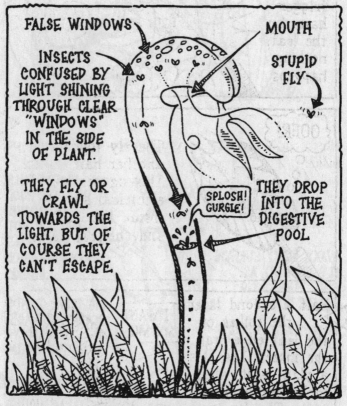

FALSE WINDOWS

MOUTH

INSECTS CONFUSED BY LIGHT SHINING THROUGH CLEAR "WINDOWS" IN THE SIDE OF PLANT.

STUPID FLY

THEY FLY OR CRAWL TOWARDS THE LIGHT, BUT OF COURSE THEY CAN'T ESCAPE.

SPLOSH! GURGLE!

THEY DROP INTO THE DIGESTIVE POOL

But there's one bug-eating plant that makes the rest look like a bunch of sweet little daisies...

## The Venus fly-trap

Don't panic! You won't find one of these lurking at the bottom of your garden. They only grow in the swamps of North and South Carolina, USA. Here's how they catch their prey...

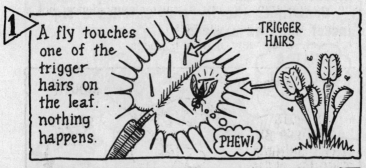

**1** A fly touches one of the trigger hairs on the leaf... nothing happens. TRIGGER HAIRS PHEW!

**2** OOER! The fly touches another hair. Yikes! This causes an electrical signal inside the leaf and the leaf folds.

**3** Half a second later ... the spikes on the leaf edge trap the insect. Yes, it's a plant with what looks like a pair of jaws. The fly is trapped! I WANT MY MUM! MUNCH!

Within half an hour the fly is squeezed tight by the leaves. Then it's digested while it's still alive! The vicious vegetable takes two weeks to complete its murderous meal.

Sometimes the fly-trap catches a big insect such as a wasp.

WHAT A WHOPPER!

BUZZ BUZZ

But the insect is too big to digest. The fly-trap runs out of digestive juice. Bacteria eat the insect's dead body and they kill the leaf as well. But the fly-trap lives to bite another day.

ERK!

*Bet you never knew!*
*Naturalist Charles Darwin (1809-1882) was a big fan of the Venus fly-trap. In the 1870s he did a series of experiments with the plant and proved that it digests its victims and soaks up the juices. Darwin thought that the fly-trap, with its revolting feeding habits, was 'the most wonderful plant in the world'.*

**Vicious uses for a bug-eating plant quiz**
All around the world people have found that bug-eating plants can be useful. Which of these uses are true and which are false?

**1** Portuguese sundew plants were traditionally used in Portugal and Spain to control flies. The nice sweet smell attracts buzzing beasties in the home. The insects crawl over the sticky leaves and get covered in gluey slime. Soon their breathing holes block up and they die a horrible lingering death. TRUE/FALSE

**2** Butterwort (a sticky-leafed plant that catches insects in a similar way to a sundew) was used in many parts of Europe for catching lice that had infested people's beds. TRUE/FALSE

I SLEPT BETTER WHEN THE BED WAS INFESTED WITH LICE

**3** You can also use butterwort to curdle milk. The plant's juices make the milk clump into stringy lumps called curds that you can eat. (Careful now, don't eat the leaf by mistake!) TRUE/FALSE

**4** The trumpet pitcher got its name because it can be played just like a trumpet. In the seventeenth century musicians would play dried trumpet pitchers as a form of street entertainment. TRUE/FALSE

**5** Sundew juice squeezed from the leaves was a traditional remedy for warts and corns. You simply squeezed the juice over the warts and corns and they would dissolve like magic. TRUE/FALSE

OH WELL, THE WARTS AND CORNS HAVE GONE!

**Answers:**

**1 TRUE.** One sundew plant can catch three flies per tentacle. After that the tentacles die.

**2 TRUE.** People put butterwort leaves between the sheets. But they could cause nightmares ... would you fancy being tucked up with a bug-eating plant?

**3 TRUE.** Simply dip the leaves in milk to make the delicious stringy curds. As eaten by the Lapp people of Scandinavia.

**4 FALSE.**

**5 TRUE.** But boring scientists reckon that the remedy doesn't work. It's just a corny old wives' tale.

Now here's a use for a bug-eating plant which is all too true ... and horrible. Can you believe that some botanists have actually *drunk* the disgusting goo from a pitcher plant? If you fancy a quick swig – here's how to...

**Make your own pitcher plant cocktail**

**1** Take one pitcher plant (huge choice of sizes available)
**2** Add:

- Some digestive juices strong enough to dissolve eggs and meat.
- 20-30 half-digested bits of dead insect
- Several hundred thousand tiny swimming algae
- A few worms
- Tadpoles
- A family of red spiders

(The last four manage to live in the fluid without getting digested.)

**3** Mix well. Leave for a few days. Serve warm.

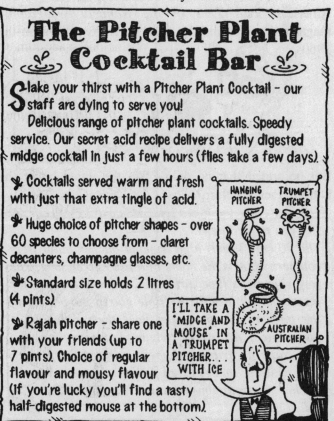

# The Pitcher Plant Cocktail Bar

**S**lake your thirst with a Pitcher Plant Cocktail – our staff are dying to serve you!

Delicious range of pitcher plant cocktails. Speedy service. Our secret acid recipe delivers a fully digested midge cocktail in just a few hours (flies take a few days).

✿ Cocktails served warm and fresh with just that extra tingle of acid.

✿ Huge choice of pitcher shapes – over 60 species to choose from – claret decanters, champagne glasses, etc.

✿ Standard size holds 2 litres (4 pints).

✿ Rajah pitcher – share one with your friends (up to 7 pints). Choice of regular flavour and mousy flavour (if you're lucky you'll find a tasty half-digested mouse at the bottom).

HANGING PITCHER

TRUMPET PITCHER

AUSTRALIAN PITCHER

I'LL TAKE A "MIDGE AND MOUSE" IN A TRUMPET PITCHER... WITH ICE

Here's what the scientists had to say…

British naturalist Alfred Wallace (1823-1913) said:

> We found it very palatable, though rather warm, and we all quenched our thirst from these natural jugs.

American Paul Zahl of the *National Geographic* magazine drank from the plant on an expedition in the 1960s:

> It tasted good though warm.

But he added that he didn't like the gluey bit at the bottom. Fancy a slurp?

*Bet you never knew!*
*The 90 cm (3 feet) high trumpet pitcher plant from southern USA is the home of a little green frog. The frog spends its time lurking in ambush. It waits for insects to fall into the horrible goo at the bottom of the pitcher. The frog then licks them up with its disgusting long, sticky tongue. But sometimes the frog loses its grip on slippery sides of the pitcher, falls in itself, and ends up getting digested. For the pitcher this must be like ten Christmas dinners all rolled into one.*

**Terrible table manners**

Fancy sharing your home with a bug-eating plant? Not any more, you don't.

**HORRIBLE HEALTH WARNING!**

Reading this section aloud at mealtimes can seriously damage your chances of getting birthday or Christmas presents for about 100 years.

**1** Some insect grubs can survive living in the pitcher plant's deadly ooze. They feed off the bits of insect body in the pitcher and seem quite happy with their horrible home. In some plants these grubs are in turn eaten by larger grubs.

**2** The pitcher doesn't mind these lodgers – in fact their disgusting droppings are rich in nitrates and they all go to feed the plant. And the grubs that eat bits of insect help to keep the pitcher clean and tidy.

**3** The twin-spurred pitcher plant goes one better by providing a cosy little room for a gang of ants. The ants guzzle some of the pitcher's victims but some insect bits plop back into the pool. And when they're cut up they're easier to digest.

**4** Some vicious seeds also eat bugs. Sounds bizarre, doesn't it? Well, get this. Shepherd's purse seeds swell up with water until their outer covering bursts open. Underneath there's a slimy layer. From now on any bug that bumps into the seed gets stuck in the slime and slowly digested. The seedling grows and grows – nourished by its tasty new food supply.

**5** The most surprising thing about bug-eating plants is that they don't really need to eat bugs at all! Deprived of their insect food they don't die they just stop growing.

But plants aren't just vicious to bugs. They're vicious to one another too. Warning! Readers looking at the next chapter might find themselves turning a sickly green colour. (If you are affected place a wastepaper basket over your head and no one will notice.)

Read on ... at your peril!

I FIND THE CLASSROOM LIGHTS TOO BRIGHT, SIR

...AND MY HEAD FEELS COLD, SIR

# VICIOUS BATTLING VEG

OW!

You might think it's easy being a plant – but it's not. Life is tough and it *can* be murder. At best, it's a jungle out there and life is one long vicious battle for survival. The signs are everywhere. Look closely at this leaf and you'll see the horrible ravages of hordes of peckish bugs and foul fungi.

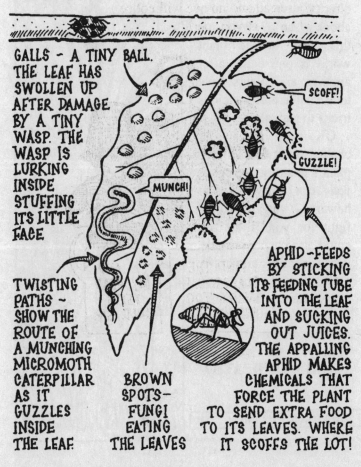

GALLS – A TINY BALL. THE LEAF HAS SWOLLEN UP AFTER DAMAGE BY A TINY WASP. THE WASP IS LURKING INSIDE STUFFING ITS LITTLE FACE

SCOFF!

GUZZLE!

MUNCH!

TWISTING PATHS – SHOW THE ROUTE OF A MUNCHING MICROMOTH CATERPILLAR AS IT GUZZLES INSIDE THE LEAF.

BROWN SPOTS – FUNGI EATING THE LEAVES

APHID –FEEDS BY STICKING ITS FEEDING TUBE INTO THE LEAF AND SUCKING OUT JUICES. THE APPALLING APHID MAKES CHEMICALS THAT FORCE THE PLANT TO SEND EXTRA FOOD TO ITS LEAVES. WHERE IT SCOFFS THE LOT!

## The jungle of death quiz

Just imagine you're a plant. So you thought plants have it easy just sitting around in the soil all day, waiting for the rain to rain and the sun to shine. You thought they didn't have to worry about a thing? Well, get this. Life in the plant world is one battle after another, and plants have to use some pretty vicious tricks to stay alive.

OK, now here's your chance to put yourself in a plant's position and see if *you* can survive. But beware – you'll have to fight for your life! You could see savage snails, insect invaders and crafty caterpillars. Are you ready? Remember, there's no peeping at the answers and no going back!

**Will you survive THE JUNGLE OF DEATH?**

70

**1** Watch out! There's a huge savage slimy snail rasping its jaws on the underside of your leaves. What do you do?

**a)** Make slippery slime under the leaves. The snails would slide off your leaves.

**b)** Grow spikes on the undersides of your leaves to neatly kebab the snail.

**c)** Allow the snails to feed. Don't panic! The snails will never eat all your leaves and what's left will grow again.

**2** Cut-throat caterpillars are crunching your leaves. If you don't stop them they'll eat you alive. What's your plan?

**a)** Drop off the affected leaves – that'll take the caterpillars with them. And good riddance!

**b)** Grow extra-thick leaves. The leaves would be too thick and chewy for the caterpillars to bite through.

**c)** Make a gas. It's an SOS signal to passing wasps.

**3** You're surrounded! On every side there are insects that want to eat your leaves. You've got to raise your own army to fight them off. Which are the best creatures to use? Better decide right now!

**a)** Ants – good for attack.

**b)** Woodlice – good for defence.

**c)** Rats – bigger than insects.

**4** Action stations – DANGER! A vicious half-starved rabbit is attacking your leaves! How can you fight it off?
**a)** Quickly grow a tendril. The wind will make the tendril wave around. This will frighten off the furry monster.
**b)** Open your flowers suddenly to scare it away.
**c)** Hit back. Sting the rabbit on the nose.

**5** You've got time to think about this one. Some bugs have laid their eggs on you. These eggs are like little ticking time bombs. In the spring the eggs will hatch and the bugs will start stuffing themselves on your tender spring leaves. What's your plan?
**a)** Don't produce any new leaves in the spring.
**b)** Produce new leaves unexpectedly early or unexpectedly late so the bugs don't know when to hatch.
**c)** Make poisons in the new leaves.

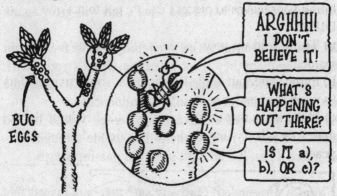

**6** Danger from the air! They're landing. An army of aphids. They've come to suck juices from your leaves. You've only got minutes to fight back. Quick, what will you do?
**a)** Send extra juices to your outer leaves so the aphids go and feed there. Then set up an ambush.

**b)** Send extra juices to the leaves where the aphids are feeding. The aphids will drink until they swell up and go pop. It's messy but deadly.

**c)** Pump the juices out of your leaves. The aphids will go away because they will have nothing to feed on. That's right, starve them into surrender.

**7** More insect invaders are marching up your stem. This time they're beetles and they mean business. They're biting your leaves to pieces. You've got to act now . . . or DIE!

**a)** Try to fold up your leaves so the beetles get trapped inside.

**b)** Pump water out of the tiny holes in your leaves and try to wash the beetles away.

**c)** Make a gas that smells like a female beetle. If they're males they'll try and find the female and leave you in peace.

**Answers:**

**1 b)** If you were an Amazon water lily you'd do this to water snails. Spikes are a good way to beat off hungry animals. Tropical screw pines have sword-shaped leaves. The barbs on the leaves mean that any creature that gets too close gets skewered. Even ordinary grass has tiny blades made from a chemical called silica. That's why careless humans sometimes cut themselves on grass.

IT'S **YOU** WHO WAS SUPPOSED TO BE CUTTING THE **GRASS**

**2 c)** Rose bushes defend themselves in this way. The wasps scoop up the caterpillars and take them back to their nest. There the caterpillars are torn apart and fed to the wasp grubs as a tasty tea-time treat. That'll teach them.

**3 a)** Ants are ideal. The South American ant plant actually provides a cosy little chamber inside its stem for the ants to live. The plant eats the ants' droppings and the ants kill any insect that comes near. So everyone's happy – except the insects that get killed.

**4 c)** Stinging nettles do this. Their leaves are covered in tiny hairs. If the hairs are touched poison pours out. A rabbit's nose is very sensitive and rather than risk a sting the cowardly bunnies avoid the nettle. In fact, dead nettles (which don't have a sting) keep the bunnies at bay and avoid getting eaten because they look like stinging nettles. It's a vicious disguise.

**5 b)** You have to be a viciously cunning oak tree to make this work. The bugs never know when there'll be leaves to eat. If the bugs hatch out too soon they'll starve and if they arrive too late the oak leaves will have had time to make poisons to defend themselves. (So there's half a point for **c**).)

**6 a)** It's a vicious trick. High flying ladybirds can spot the aphids on the outer leaves and chew them up for supper. And serves 'em right!

**7c)** This is a typically vicious trick by the cucumber plant. The cunning cucumber keeps its cool and the bothered beetles beat it.

*Now add up your score…*
Give yourself *one* point for each correct answer.
**Score 5-7.** YOU HAVE CONQUERED THE JUNGLE OF DEATH. Congratulations! You'd make a blooming brilliant plant. Nothing can touch you – the insect invaders don't stand a chance.
**Score 3-4.** Although you have a budding talent you're still a bit green. With a bit of luck you'll live to grow another day.
**Score 1-2.** You won't last long in the jungle of death. You're not vicious enough – better stick to being a human.

## Teacher's tea-break teaser

Hammer boldly on the staffroom door. When your teacher comes to the door smile sweetly and enquire:

YOU KNOW THAT YOUR TEA CONTAINS TANNIN – WHAT DOES YOUR TANNIN DO TO AN INSECT'S MOUTH PARTS?

ERK!

**Answer:**
Tannins are bitter chemicals made by many types of plant including roses, oak trees and tea plants. They protect the plant from aphids. The tannins gum up an aphid's mouth parts so it starves to death. Although tannins also give its tea its slightly bitter taste, they don't gum up human mouth parts – worse luck. If they did your teacher would be speechless after every tea-break.

*Bet you never knew!*
*On top of all their other problems plants can also be attacked by viruses. These tiny objects are far smaller even than bacteria. They're the same things that give you colds and 'flu. Plants get them from the bites of hungry bugs like aphids. But they don't get blocked or runny noses or sneezing – oh no. It's far worse. If a virus such as mosaic leaf attacks our cucumber plant (see page 40) its leaves would become discoloured and it would die. There's no cure!*

And if that isn't bad enough some vicious vegetables are keen to make a meal of any plant that gets in their way. These plants are REALLY VILLAINOUS!

# VEGETABLE VILLAINS I HAVE KNOWN

## THE CASE NOTES OF CHIEF INSPECTOR GARDEN

Whenever I look at these notes I am shocked by the sheer inventiveness and viciousness of these vegetable villains. Clearly society should not tolerate these vegetable riff-raff.

**NAME: the Strangler Fig**

**LAST SEEN:** South America

**KNOWN CRIMES:** strangling trees One day I came across the dead body of a mature tree. I deduced immediately that foul play was involved and I was soon proved right. On closer examination I realized that the cause of death was due to strangulation and thirst and the blocking of light. It seems that the victim was powerless to run away or hide.

**METHODS USED:** The villainous vegetable had climbed up the tree and wrapped its branches around the victim's trunk tighter and tighter.

TREE

ROOT

STRANGLER FIG

I CAN'T BREATH!

Five years later it had sunk its roots into the ground and stolen the victim's water supply. It must have been a terrible way to grow - er, go.

UNFORTUNATE VICTIM

ARGHH!

**NAME: Dodder**

**LAST SEEN:** sightings reported worldwide

**KNOWN CRIMES:** murdering countless plants

DODDER

**METHODS USED:** the dodder usually loiters in the undergrowth. Waiting for a victim, I shouldn't wonder. Then quite without warning the victim is grabbed by the dodder's tendrils. The victim is usually then stabbed in several places by the tendrils which suck out its insides. A most vicious criminal.

**NAME:** The Corpse Flower
(alias the Indian pipe)

**LAST SEEN:** lurking in the forests of north-west America

**DESCRIPTION:** ghostly pale and corpse-like, 25cm (10 inches) high

**KNOWN CRIMES:** its roots make unprovoked attacks on harmless underground fungi and suck out their juices.

**METHODS USED:** my enquiries have established that the crime occurs because water in the fungi juices is quite naturally drawn towards the thicker liquid in the corpse flower's roots by a natural process, called osmosis (os-mo-sis). Be that as it may – this villain is deadly.

I HAD TO GET TO THE ROOT OF THE PROBLEM...

SLURP!

SUCK!

79

**NAME:** Christmas tree

(Note: The name is due to the fact that the tree flowers around Christmas. But the public should be warned this is no ordinary Christmas tree. Members of the public are requested not to place presents under it. The villain will probably try to eat them.)

**LAST SEEN:** Western Australia

**DESCRIPTION:** a tree with pretty orange or gold flowers. Many people have been fooled by this pretty, innocent exterior.

**KNOWN CRIMES:** roots seek out roots of other plants.

**METHODS USED:** Woody fangs sink into other plant roots followed by the tubes that divert the other plant's water into the Christmas tree.

Beware: this character is dangerous – approach with extreme caution. Has even been known to attack underground phone cables.

**The secret diary of a killer cucumber**

Now you might think that faced with a vicious killer plant the other plants might curl up and die. Well, surely they're defenceless, aren't they? Not necessarily. Some plants fight back. Take the cucumber plant we were looking at earlier, for example. It looks harmless enough, but appearances can be deceptive. Just imagine if it could keep a diary of its life. OK, so you're *really* going to have to stretch your imagination for this.

Here's what it might say…

## Spring –April

This is disgraceful. The gardener's gone and planted me outside. Next to all these bullying geranium plants. I want to go back to that nice warm greenhouse.

ARGH!

Blast him!

**Two days later…**

The geraniums are trying to get me. Their roots are pumping out poison gas. Lucky all this gas doesn't harm me. It's all to do with the incredible mix of chemicals in my roots that can soak up poisons and re-use them.

But I'm still not putting up with it!
I'm going to swallow up
the gas in my roots.
That'll sort 'em!

TEE HEE

me

**A few hours later...**
Now I'll get my revenge. I'll make the
geraniums' gas into
a more deadly mixture
of my own. And send it
right back to them.

ARGH!

**Two weeks later...**
I don't like the way those tomatoes
are looking at me. Their roots are
taking too much water from
the soil. It's got to stop.

**Three hours later...** The enemy
This will teach them. The soil is full of
tiny nematode worms. Ugly little brutes.
The soil is too dry for them to be
active so they're asleep at the
moment. This gas will wake them
up. The worms don't like the gas
so they slither towards the
tomatoes. Yeah, go get 'em, you worms.

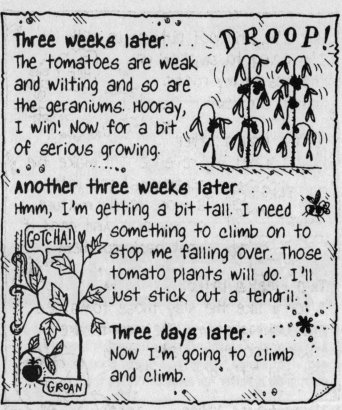

**Three weeks later...** ~DROOP!~
The tomatoes are weak and wilting and so are the geraniums. Hooray, I win! Now for a bit of serious growing.

**Another three weeks later...**
Hmm, I'm getting a bit tall. I need something to climb on to stop me falling over. Those tomato plants will do. I'll just stick out a tendril.

GOTCHA!

GROAN

**Three days later...**
Now I'm going to climb and climb.

## Dare you discover ... how to make a plant attack you?

*What you need:*
A lot of bravery
A pea plant, our pet cucumber plant,
a passion flower or any plant with tendrils
A pencil

*What you do:*
Gently stroke the tip of the tendril with the pencil.

*What does the tendril do?*

**a)** It grabs the pencil and snaps it in half.

**b)** The tendril draws back suddenly.

**c)** It slowly bends.

**Answer:**

**c)** The tendril is making ready to coil around the pencil. It thinks the pencil is another plant stalk. Within a few hours the centre of the tendril will coil like a telephone flex and pull the entire plant towards the pencil.

# HORRIBLE HEALTH WARNING!

**D**on't be too slow. If you hang around for more than a few days the plant will twine its tendrils around your neck. That's what happens to a nearby plant as the tendril plant grabs it. Better run away before it's too late.

*Bet you never knew!*

*One good way for a plant to defend itself against insects or animals is to make itself poisonous so it can't be eaten. Do you like the lovely, cool, refreshing taste of mint? Its flavour is actually due to a poison in the leaf that affects your nerves. Of course, it's not strong enough to harm you. It just switches on the nerves that sense cool things on your tongue. So that everything tastes cool and refreshing. But for insects the chemicals are just too poisonous and they die.*

**A few things you should know about vicious plant poisons. Here is the news.**

**THE BAD NEWS**

SOME PLANT POISONS ARE DEADLY POISONOUS TO HUMANS AND THEY HAVE HORRIBLE EFFECTS ON THE BODY

**THE GOOD NEWS**

MOST PLANT POISONS ARE DESIGNED TO BUMP OFF INSECTS. THEY'RE NOT SO HARMFUL TO US. IN FACT, A TINY DOSE OF SOME POISONS CAN BE GOOD FOR YOU. THEY CAN BE MADE INTO USEFUL MEDICINES

The calabar bean was once used in trials. The accused person had to eat the poisonous bean. If they died they were considered guilty, if they lived they were innocent. Of course, the bean had no idea whether or not you deserved to die. The trick was to gulp it down and then sick it up again before the poison had a chance to work.

P-PLEASE, DON'T MAKE ME...

**EAT IT!** OR YOU WON'T GET ANY PUDDING

The mandrake root is poisonous. There were once a lot of strange superstitions about it because it looked a bit like a man. One idea was that the mandrake screams when it's dug up. In Roman times dogs were used to dig up the roots because the Romans thought anyone who heard the mandrake's scream would die.

Deadly nightshade is also known as "belladonna" which means "beautiful lady". This is because women used to put the poison in their eyes to make their pupils (the black bits in the centre of the eye) bigger and more beautiful. *Don't* try this at home. Oddly enough, a tiny drop is used today to make a drug that widens the pupils during eye surgery.

BEAUTIFUL   DEAD BEAUTIFUL   DEAD

The poison curare comes from the bark and roots of the strychnos (strick-nos) tree. It's used by native Americans to tip their deadly arrows and it works in seconds. Oddly enough a little curare is used to relax a patient's muscles during operations on the guts.

And talking about poisonous plant drugs...

## Hall of fame: William Withering (1741-1799)
Nationality: British

William was rich, bad-tempered and boring. Although he worked as a doctor his favourite hobby was botany. In 1776 he wrote a massive, boring book that described hundreds of species of British plants. (William's other hobbies were dog breeding and playing the flute – but they aren't relevant to our story.)

Naturally, William had lots of scientist pals. They all used to meet together on nights of the full moon and called themselves the Lunar Society. It was a sensible arrangement because they could all see their way home by the light of the moon but local people called them "lunar-tics" because of their odd ideas.

YOU'VE HEARD OF SUNDIALS – WELL, I'VE INVENTED A MOONDIAL.

HE CALLS IT A 'LUNAR-TIC-TOC'

William had a few of these himself. He was convinced that the poison from foxgloves could cure the deadly disease dropsy. Foxglove is a pretty pink flower about 1.5 metres (5 feet) high. It was also known as "bloody man's fingers" and "dead man's bells". Why? Because foxglove is deadly poisonous. So how could a poison be a medicine? Here's the story of William's great discovery.

One day he visited an old woman who was sick with dropsy. "I'll be better soon," she cackled, "thanks to my secret herb tea."

William was too polite to say, "What a load of old rubbish – you're a gonner I fear, my dear."

But that's what he probably thought. After all, dropsy

was a very painful disease that made the lower body swell up to horrible proportions. There was no known cure.

But the next week the old woman was skipping about the house and getting on with a bit of spring cleaning. William was gobsmacked and insisted on buying some of the amazing tea for further study.

CUP OF TEA, MR WITHERING?

He found out that the active ingredient was foxglove leaves. Only a small bit, not enough to kill the person who drank it. So he tested foxglove tea on some of his patients. He noted one particular case of a retired builder with dropsy…

… HIS BELLY SUBSIDED AND IN ABOUT TEN DAYS HE BEGAN TO EAT WITH A HEARTY APPETITE.

There were only two little difficulties...

**1** People who took the treatment found their heartbeat very fast and they wanted to pee all the time.

**2** If you took too much foxglove you died. One famous victim was the former prime minister Charles James Fox (1749-1806), who died after a cure went wrong. So you could say, "foiled physicians failed to fix Fox with foxgloves".

In 1785, William Withering wrote a book about the foxglove and doctors began to use it more and more. Today, a drug called digitalis which is made from foxgloves is used to treat people with a fluttering heart beat. And that's lucky 'cos you'll need to be in good heart for the next chapter. It's foul enough to set your pulse racing.

It really stinks...

# Foul fungi

If plants are vicious, fungi are – well, super vicious. In fact, the only people who like fungi are gourmets who like to eat them and botanists who like to study them.

HAVE YOU FINISHED WITH IT YET? I'M STARVING!

So what do you think? Are fungi really that bad? Well, yes, they are. Read on and find out why...

## Vicious veg fact file

NAME: Fungi

THE BASIC FACTS: 1 Fungi aren't real plants. They have no stems, no roots and they don't make food by photosynthesis.

2 Unlike plants they don't contain cellulose (that's the stuff in roughage, remember). Instead, they are made up of chitin (kitin). By some weird coincidence this is also the chemical that makes up insects' jaws.

**THE VICIOUS DETAILS:** Fungi feed by:

🍄 Sticking feeding tubes called hyphae into their food.

🍄 Making an acid that dissolves the food.

🍄 Sucking up the juices.
Sometimes the "food" is a living plant or animal.
Some plants fight back. If they sense the acid, they grow extra thick roots or leaves so the hyphae can't break in.

## Dare you discover ... how to grow your own fungi?

*What you need is:*
A slice of white bread
A little water
A clear polythene bag

*What you do is:*
**1** Sprinkle a little water on the bread so it's slightly moist.
**2** Place the bread in the bag and seal it tightly.
**3** Leave the bread in a warm place for 2-3 days.

*What do you notice?*
If you're lucky you should find some grey-green fungi growing on the bread. Where do you think it came from?
**a)** The bread
**b)** The bag
**c)** The air in the bag

**Answer:**
c) Probably. As you're about to find out fungi grow
from spores and they're everywhere. So there were
probably a few spores in the air that went into the bag.
Throw the bag away unopened – you don't want your
fungi to invade your packed lunch, do you?

**Everything you always wanted to know about fungi
but were afraid to ask**

**1** Fungi spread by making spores that are just blobs made
of single cells.

**2** Many fungi grow the strange objects we call toadstools
in order to spread the spores.

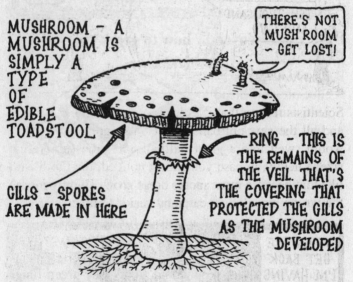

MUSHROOM – A
MUSHROOM IS
SIMPLY A
TYPE
OF
EDIBLE
TOADSTOOL

THERE'S NOT
MUSH'ROOM
– GET LOST!

RING – THIS IS
THE REMAINS OF
THE VEIL. THAT'S
THE COVERING THAT
PROTECTED THE GILLS
AS THE MUSHROOM
DEVELOPED

GILLS – SPORES
ARE MADE IN HERE

**3** Spores get everywhere. In fact, for each 0.76 cubic
metres (1 cubic yard) of air you're breathing at the
moment there are at least 10,000 spores floating around.
And they're tough. Just look at what they can survive…

- Boiling water
- Freezing
- Floating in the sea
- Floating in the air as high as a jet airliner

**4** Fungi make huge amounts of spores. Some mushrooms produce 10,000,000,000 (ten thousand million) spores in a few days. But that's nothing… The giant puffball fungus can swell to 2.64 metres (8 feet 8 inches) across. From a distance you could mistake it for a huge dead sheep. It makes 5,000,000,000,000 (five thousand billion) spores in less than three months. If you don't believe me, just try counting them.

Scientists reckon that if every spore grew into a puffball and all the new puffballs' spores also grew – the Earth would swell into a giant puffball 800 times its present size! Luckily, in case you hadn't noticed, the Earth isn't like that because most spores don't grow. They end up in the wrong place or get eaten by various tiny creatures.

**5** Fungi aren't fussy about what they have for lunch. Quite the opposite – they scoff everything and anything. Different species of fungi can digest:

• Petrol
• Cows droppings*
• Camera lenses
• Plastic

* This foul fungus allows its spores to blow over grass. Cows eat the grass and the spores come out with the droppings. And new fungi feast on the delicious dung.

Wonder if they could manage a school dinner...

**6** Some vicious fungi catch and eat living animals. A species of underground fungi makes little hoops.

It also makes a chemical that encourages soil creatures called eel worms to wriggle into the hoop.

The hoop swells, trapping the eel worm. Hypahe grow into the victim's body and suck out the delicious juices.

## Could you be a scientist?

You're out for a walk in the woods and you notice a fairy ring – that's a circle of toadstools. Can you work out how this circle came to be formed?

Clue – it wasn't planted by fairies.

AND IT WASN'T MADE FOR TOADS TO SIT ON

GOOD TO SEE YOU, BILL

YEAH, IT'S NICE TO HAVE A NATTER, JACK

**a)** The toadstools were planted by animals. The fact that they form a circle is a complete coincidence.

**b)** The fairy ring grew outwards as underground hyphae spread out from a single spore.

**c)** The fairy ring is growing inwards. The fungi can tell where each other are and they're trying to bunch together for protection.

---

**Answer:**

**b)** The larger the ring the older the fungus. Bet you never knew the largest living thing on Earth is a fungus. In 1992 scientists found the honey fungus in Washington State, USA. It covered 600 hectares (1,480 acres) – that's the size of 556 football pitches!

Scientists reckon the monster fungus could be over 700 years old. 

MAKES ME FEEL YOUNG!

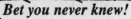

*Bet you never knew!*

*Fungi use smell to attract flies. True to its name, the stinkhorn fungus pongs like rotten meat mixed with a blocked toilet. (Phwoar!) You might not appreciate the perfume but flies and slugs love it. They guzzle the fungus cap and distribute the spores in their disgusting droppings.*

Other anti-social fungi include:

● The stinker toadstool. Pongs like coal gas.

● The russula (rus-sel-a) fungus. Reeks of rotting fish.

● A species of boletus (bo-leet-us) fungus. A scientist said that one sickening whiff of this one made him throw up.

**Vicious veg expressions**

Is this fatal?

## Foul fungi – the good, the bad and the ugly
## The good

**1** The fungus called "lawyer's wig" drips out its spores mixed with a black slime. This is a good source of ink and was once used by country people although it's a bit smelly.

**2** Fly agaric toadstools were considered a good fly killer. A bit of skin from the toadstool was left in a saucer of milk. The flies drank the milk and died. But don't touch the fungus yourself because it's a good human-killer too.

**3** Forty species of tropical fungi make good night lights. They use chemical reactions to glow after dark with an eerie blue-green light. Nobody knows why they do it. Maybe it's so nightclubbing insects can dine out on their spores.

## The bad

These fungi are dressed to kill…

**1 The death cap toadstool**

Kills 90 per cent of humans stupid enough to eat it. The poisons make the gut all blistered. It's no fun. The victim chucks up all the time until their body dries out, their liver swells up and their heart stops beating. If one of these turns up on your pizza RUN FOR IT!

**2 Ergots**

These little fungi grow on wet rye. Sound harmless enough, don't they? Er – no. Anyone who eats ergots suffers from a deadly condition called St Anthony's Fire. The effects include madness, throwing up and a burning pain in the bum. Their fingers and toes turn rotten and then drop off. Yep. One dose of that could spoil your whole day.*

* Don't panic – you won't find ergots lurking in your rye crispbread sandwich. Nowadays rye crops are treated with chemicals called fungicides to kill off the ergots.

## The ugly

No fungus would win a beauty contest. But this lot could win an Oscar in a horror movie.

**1 Dead man's foot**

A brown lumpy fungus. It starts off below ground and works its way to the surface where it does a weird impression of a rotting human foot. It smells of mushrooms and, surprisingly, it doesn't taste too bad. Anyone fancy a nibble?

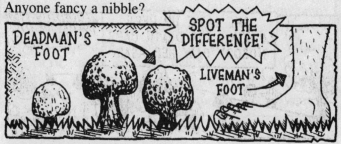

**2 Dead man's fingers**

Grows in the woods of Europe, North America and Asia. Clumps of black bloated objects poking out of the soil. Guess what they remind people of? Scientists aren't sure if this fungus is good to eat, so who knows? Maybe it's finger-lickin' good. Or dead rotten.

**3 The ox-tongue fungus**

Grows on oak and chestnut trees in Europe, North America and Asia. Looks just like a tongue sticking out of a tree trunk. And guess what – if you cut it, red stuff dribbles out. Some brave people have tried the fungus and reported that it has a horrible sharp taste. So, I suppose you could call it a sharp-tongued fungus. Ha ha.

*Bet you never knew!*
*But there's one fungus that has caused more deaths than the deadliest toadstool. Potato blight Phytophthora (fi-toff thaw-ra) and its favourite food (amazingly enough) is – potatoes. The fungus can turn a whole field of potatoes into a black stinking mess. Unfortunately, in Ireland in 1845 many people lived off potatoes and had little else to eat. So when the blight swept across Ireland around half a million people starved to death.*

## Foul edible fungi

Things were so desperate during the Irish famine that the people ate stinging nettles, weeds and seaweed. Of course, there was something else they might have eaten. Fungi. After all, mushrooms are fungi, and some types can be quite a delicacy. Oh yes – it's true...

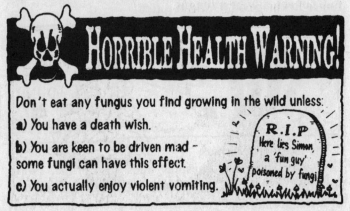

HORRIBLE HEALTH WARNING!

Don't eat any fungus you find growing in the wild unless:

a) You have a death wish.

b) You are keen to be driven mad – some fungi can have this effect.

c) You actually enjoy violent vomiting.

R.I.P
Here lies Simon,
a 'fun guy'
poisoned by fungi

## Foul fungal foods

**1** So you like mushroom soup? Better tuck in before you read this next bit. The term "mushroom" actually has no scientific meaning – it just means a fungus that you can eat. Growing in the dark and feeding on rotting manure is the ideal life for a mushroom.

**2** Truffles are smelly underground fungi that look like lumps of coal. So it's strange to think that some people like to eat them. They're a real delicacy in posh restaurants. Truffles can sell for over £1,000 a kilogram. Truffles are traditionally dug up by pigs that eat the fungus and spread the spores in their droppings. But with prices like that the poor old pigs that sniff out truffles for reastaurants probably never get to eat any.

**3** Of course, some fungi fans will kill for a taste of their favourite fungi. Kill themselves, that is. Take false morel, for example. This is a horrible-looking fungus that looks like a lump of poo and grows in woods in Europe. It's actually poisonous but it can be eaten if it's first very thoroughly boiled to destroy the poisons. Don't try this at home, kids – for one thing, that poo-like lump you find may not actually be a fungus.

**4**. The plum and custard fungus grow on rotten old pine stumps. Sounds rather delicious, doesn't it? If you like plums and custard. In fact, the name doesn't come from its taste but from its yellow and plum colouring. And although it can be eaten this fungus tastes and smells like rotten old wood.

So you'd have to be as thick as a rotten plank to try it.

### Four not-so-foul fungi facts

Is your teacher a mycologist?*

\* That's a scientist who studies fungi.

If so they might try to persuade you that fungi are really quite friendly and cuddly. And bamboozle you with facts like these:

**1** Some fungi kill harmful bacteria. In 1928, Scottish scientist Alexander Fleming (1881-1955) noticed a fungus called penicillium (pen-ni-silli-um) growing on the special lab plates he'd used to grow bacteria on. The scientist had gone on holiday without cleaning the plates properly, and the fungus had killed the bacteria. (Don't get any ideas from this – leaving the washing up for a few weeks won't guarantee a major scientific discovery.)

**2** Fleming discovered the fungus that made the germ-killing substance called penicillin. In the Second World War, Australian scientist Howard Florey (1898-1968) and German-born Ernst Chain (1906-1979) found out how to make the drug in large amounts. And US drugs companies made the penicillin that saved the lives of thousands of soldiers.

**3** Fungi help plants. If fungi didn't eat dead wood the stuff would just pile up and get in the way of growing plants. That's because plants can't scoff wood – well, wooden you just know it! So the fungi take in valuable chemicals from the wood and, when the fungi die and rot, these chemicals can provide food for plants and animals.

**4** Friendly fungi also feed plants more directly. About three-quarters of all plants have fungi clinging to their roots. These fungi – called mycorrhizae (my-cor-ritz-y) – take in minerals and pass them on to the roots. In return they take some sugars from the roots. So it's fair exchange and everyone wins.

On that happy note let's look at some flowers. This is Horrible Science, of course, so the flowers in the next chapter aren't all pretty and sweet smelling. Some of them are hideously ugly and make such an appalling pong that you might want to throw up. So you'll need a clothes peg on your nose before you begin to read!

DAT'S BEDDA!

# Fiendish flowers

There's something about flowers that make some humans go all gooey and soppy.

Or make up silly poems…

But the vicious truth is that no plant has ever made flowers in order to cheer up humans. The plants are keener to impress insects and bats and other creatures for reasons you're about to find out. And these vicious vegetables are quite capable of using low-down dirty tricks to achieve their aim… pollination.

**Vicious veg fact file**

NAME: Pollination

THE BASIC FACTS: Pollination is how flowers make seeds. It's a straightforward job.

**1** You make pollen in your flowers. See page 107 for the details.

**2** You transfer some of your pollen to another plant of your species. OK so far?

**3** Then the other plant makes seeds that grow into baby plants. Easy-peasy.

THE VICIOUS DETAILS: All this pollen flying about can give people a stinking dose of hay fever. See page 117 for the grisly details.

HOW'S THE HAY FEVER?

DOT DOO BAD

### Flowers – the inside story

**1** The easiest way for a plant to spread pollen around is to let the wind blow it away. Plants such as grasses and willow trees grow big feathery stigmas to catch the pollen and dangle them out of their flowers.

**2** Most flowering plants use animals to take their pollen from one plant to another. But first they need to grab the animal's attention. And for this they need PUBLICITY. Yes, we're talking about razzmatazz – flowers, colours, perfumes – the works!

**3** Next they need sticky nectar to feed the animals. I mean, they're not going to shift pollen out of the goodness of their little hearts, are they?

**4** Plants employ a surprising range of creatures. There are flies, beetles, hummingbirds, bats – yes, bats. (Some tropical flowers open at night so bats can pollinate them.)

**5** To show how it actually works we took this cute little flower…

and hacked it in half…

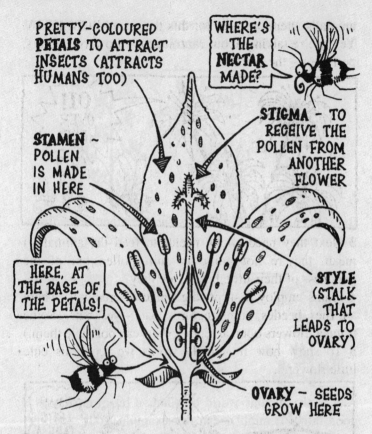

PRETTY-COLOURED **PETALS** TO ATTRACT INSECTS (ATTRACTS HUMANS TOO)

WHERE'S THE **NECTAR** MADE?

**STAMEN** ~ POLLEN IS MADE IN HERE

**STIGMA** ~ TO RECEIVE THE POLLEN FROM ANOTHER FLOWER

HERE, AT THE BASE OF THE PETALS!

**STYLE** (STALK THAT LEADS TO OVARY)

**OVARY** ~ SEEDS GROW HERE

But hold on – why do plants go to all this bother?

**Why don't plants go in for DIY pollination?**
Yes. Why don't plants just pollinate themselves? In fact, some flowers do and yes, it really is much less fuss. But it's much better to get another plant involved. Here's why...

Pollen and the ovary cells contain chemical codes known as genes that tell the seedlings how to grow and what features to develop. If a plant pollinated itself its seedlings would get all the same codes as its parents, so they'd be identical to the parent.

But if the plant is pollinated by another plant its seedlings would take on some features of the second parent.

And in the vicious world of plants a bit of variety is a good thing. It might mean, for example, your seedlings grow up with some vital feature like a few sharp spikes or a deadlier poison to help keep those peckish rabbits at bay.

### How to pollinate a plant in three easy stages
Every species of plant makes different-shaped pollen grains. When a pollen grain lands on a flower's stigma the flower senses that the pollen is the right species. Some flowers can sense that the pollen is not one of its own grains. It may be able to feel the shape of the pollen grain or it might be able to recognize chemicals from the

grain. No one is quite sure how they do it. Clever, eh? Next...

**1** A little tube grows from the pollen grain and down into the ovary of the flower.

**2** A cell from the pollen grain joins up with a cell from the ovary to make a single extra-large cell.

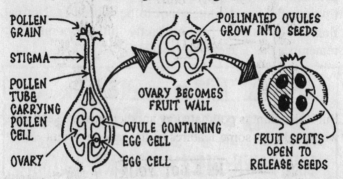

POLLEN GRAIN

STIGMA

POLLEN TUBE CARRYING POLLEN CELL

OVARY

OVULE CONTAINING EGG CELL

EGG CELL

OVARY BECOMES FRUIT WALL

POLLINATED OVULES GROW INTO SEEDS

FRUIT SPLITS OPEN TO RELEASE SEEDS

**3** This splits many times to make the seeds of the plant. Clever innit?

*Bet you never knew!*

*1 You can't rely on insects. More often than not they take pollen to another species of flower. In order to make seeds, pollen has to go to a flower belonging to its own species.*

*2 That's why many species of flowers sign up a type of insect for an exclusive deal. Their flowers are designed so only this particular insect can visit them. That way the plant can be 100 per cent sure its pollen will go to the right kind of flower! For example, one species of orchid from Madagascar has a flower 46 cm (18 inches) deep. And the nectar at the bottom can only be reached by a rare species of hawk moth with an unusually long tongue.*

Of course, the moth will then fly on to find another orchid of the same species.

But plants use plenty more vicious tricks to get pollinated. As you're about to find out. Here are a load of flowers that are definitely not to be sniffed at. Normal flower shows are full of pretty little blooms. But remember this is Horrible Science...

# 🐝 A Fiendish 🐝 Flower Show

## LOW-DOWN DIRTY TRICKS SECTION

### 3rd — The African sycamore fig (Africa)

**PLAYS TRICKS ON:** gall wasps

**LOW-DOWN DIRTY TRICKS: 1** Female wasps containing eggs and pollen force their way into the fig, losing wings on the way (ouch!).

**2** The females lay eggs in the flowers, then pollinate the stigmas. Seeds begin to develop, but grubs hatch and start eating them. (Some seeds survive, thank goodness!) Male wasps hatch first, fertilize the females before they emerge – then the males die! When the fruit ripens the female wasps escape, collecting pollen on the way to take to the next fig flower. Then it all starts again.

I'M FREE!

**110**

# The mirror orchid
## (Western Mediterranean)

**PLAYS TRICKS ON:** bees

**LOW-DOWN DIRTY TRICKS:**

**1** The flower fools male bees into thinking it's a female bee. It looks like a female bee and even smells like one.

**2** The male bee tries to give the flower a cuddle. The stamens swoop down and whack a blob of pollen on the male bee's head.

**3** The bewildered bee flies off in search of another female, and usually ends up taking pollen to another mirror orchid.

YOO HOO!

I THINK I'M IN LOVE...

THWACK

ERK!

POLLEN

YOU'LL NEVER GUESS WHAT JUST HAPPENED TO ME!

# Dead horse arum
## (Mediterranean islands)

PLAYS TRICKS ON: blow flies

LOW-DOWN DIRTY TRICKS:

**1** Looks just like rotten meat. Makes a realistic stink so flies think they can lay their eggs inside it. Even provides a hole for them to explore what looks horribly like an empty eye socket.

**2** Doesn't lay on food for the fly grubs when they hatch out. So they starve to death.

GET STUCK IN, KIDS

ROTTING MEAT STENCH

**3** Traps the female flies in the flower until its stigmas pick up any pollen the flies might be carrying. Many flies die of suffocation inside the fiendish flower. (To be fair the flower does give them some nectar to drink.)

**4** Flower only lets the flies out when they've been dusted with pollen. Ready to take to the next dead horse arum.

112

# A Fiendish Flower Show

## FREAKY FLOWERS SECTION

### Puya plant
### (Bolivia, South America)

**DON'T LIKE THE COLOUR MUCH**

**WHY DO I BOTHER?**

**APPEARANCE:** Huge head of flowers – the largest in the world. It can measure up to 10 metres (33 feet) across.

**FREAKY FEATURES:** Takes 150 years to grow to the stage where it makes flowers. Then it dies. Makes you wonder why the peculiar puya plant bothers.

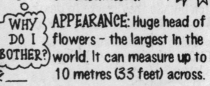

**2nd**

### Rafflesia (otherwise known as the "stinking corpse lily")
### (Borneo, Indonesia)

**APPEARANCE:** Giant orange cabbage-shaped flower up to one metre (3.5 feet) across. The first European to find it, Sir Thomas Raffles (1781–1826), called it:

**THE LARGEST AND MOST MAGNIFICENT FLOWER IN THE WORLD**

...AND ALSO THE STINKIEST FLOWER IN THE WORLD

**FREAKY FEATURES:**

**1** Grows on forest vines and sucks out their juices.

**2** Stinks of rotting flesh.

**3** It's pollinated either by flies or shrews and then rots into a black stinking mass.

WHO'RE YOU CALLING A FREAK?

# Titan arum
## (Sumatra, Indonesia)

**APPEARANCE:** Freaky. It grows to 3.7 metres (12 feet) high. The sheath that surrounds its huge spike of flowers is 91 cm (3 feet) wide.

**FREAKY FEATURES:** Take a look at the next page!

# THE TERRIBLE TITAN

BELLISIMO!

In 1878 Italian botanist Odoardo Beccari found a giant flower growing in a forest.

His assistants dug it up together with its 1.5 metres (five feet) wide corm or swollen root.

Unfortunately, they dropped the heavy plant. The corm was full of vegetable fat. It

SPLOOSH!

splattered everywhere and started to rot. Eventually Odoardo was able to send some titan arum seeds to Italy and one of the young plants that grew from the seeds ended up at Kew Gardens in London. When the flowers opened they caused a sensation and thousands flocked to see them. . .

SEEDS! WHY DIDN'T I THINK OF THAT SOONER?

# THE KEW TIMES
## 22 June 1887

# What a blooming stink!

**S**ightseers at Kew to see the titan arum were greeted by a gobsmacking stench from the fiendish flower. Said one visitor, "Phwoar - what a foul stink, worse than a pig farm it was."

Several ladies needed first aid because of the revolting reek. The sickening smell is described as being like rotten fish and burnt sugar mixed together. A botanist working in the gardens said, "The flowers are pollinated by beetles that eat rotting flesh. The beetles think the smell is heavenly.

I can't say that I agree, in fact I've got to dash. . ."

Artist Matilda Smith (1854-1926) had the unenviable job of painting the flower from close quarters. She nearly passed out from the horrible stench. Still, it could have been worse. She might have had hay fever too.

OK, SO I FOUND IT HARD TO CONCENTRATE

## Horrible hay fever

In the summer pollen gets everywhere. Wind-blown pollen has tiny air bags attached so it can fly really well. Some grains of pollen are blown 4,800 km (3,000 miles) by the wind and float 5,800 metres (19,000 feet) into the air. Oh, so you know all about that? Well, if so, chances are you suffer from hay fever. You know the signs. Watery eyes, runny nose, sneezing. It's like having a bad cold all summer long. So, who's to blame?

Well, plants obviously, because they make pollen. But it's your own body that causes the nasty effects of hay fever. When a grain of pollen floats up your nose it often sticks there. S'not fair, is it?

**117**

In a hay fever sufferer, the body sends chemicals called histamines (hiss-ta-meens) to fight off the intruder. Unfortunately, they make the area feel horribly sore and that's hay fever.

Mind you, by the end of the summer it's all over. No more smelly flowers and pesky pollen for another year. Hooray! But the plants are still hard at work. You'll have to turn to the next chapter to find out what they're up to.

# Sprouting seeds and rotting fruits

Did you know the word fruit means "enjoy" in Latin – that's the old Roman language. Yep, the Romans liked a nice bit of fruit.

But you might think fruit tastes rotten and you'd rather wear a cactus in your pants than eat a school dinner fruit salad.

Cheer up, though, 'cos with the help of some of the facts in this chapter, you might be able to argue your way out of ever having to eat another apple again!

# Vicious veg fact file

**NAME:** Fruits and seeds

**THE BASIC FACTS: 1** Fruits and seeds are designed with one aim. To make sure the seedlings of a plant grow a distance away from the parent plant. That way they won't be fighting each other for light or water.

**2** Seeds come in all shapes and sizes from orchid seeds that weigh 1 millionth of a gram to the 18 kg (40 lb) double coconut, which is also, amazingly, a seed.

**THE VICIOUS DETAILS:** Unripe fruits taste disgusting. That's the plant's way of making sure animals don't scoff the fruit before they're ripe. Some unripe fruit is even poisonous. Any animal that eats it will end up dead sorry. Well, mostly dead, actually.

> P'RHAPS I'LL LEAVE THEM FOR A FEW MORE DAYS

## Seed secrets
**1** The inside story
A seed is like a space capsule filled with everything a plant needs to survive. Take this harmless little broad bean, for example...

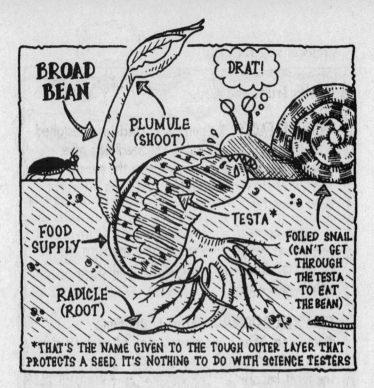

*THAT'S THE NAME GIVEN TO THE TOUGH OUTER LAYER THAT PROTECTS A SEED. IT'S NOTHING TO DO WITH SCIENCE TESTERS

**2** Get moving

Plants use loads of viciously ingenious methods to shift seeds. Here are just a few of them:

**a)** The wind. Some plants give their seeds little parachutes to help them fly. Like dandelion seeds…

121

Or little helicopter wings...

## b) Creature comforts

Animals are always on the move and always hungry. So for a plant it makes sense to get animals to shift their seeds for them.

The seeds need a nice thick testa. That'll protect them from acid juices in the animal's guts.

**Vicious veg expressions**

Did she say germs ate it?

## Strange seed stories quiz

TRUE or FALSE?

**1** As the Mediterranean squirting cucumber ripens it makes more and more slimy juice until it explodes. TRUE/FALSE

**2** The sharp hooks of the grapple plant seeds stick into an elephant's foot. They only fall off after the hook has been worn out by being walked on for quite a distance. For the elephant this vicious plant is a jumbo-sized problem. TRUE/FALSE

**3** But elephants actually help protect acacia tree seeds from beetles by eating the seeds. TRUE/FALSE

**4** Deadly nightshade berries kill the animal that eats them and the vicious seedling grows out of the dead animal's body. TRUE/FALSE

**5** Australian mistletoe seeds are spread by a bird wiping its bum on a tree. TRUE/FALSE

123

**6** The South American hura tree is known as the monkey's dinner bell because of its bell-shaped seeds. Monkeys love to eat them for dinner. TRUE/FALSE

**7** Mangrove seeds fall downwards like spears. (That's why it's not a good idea to have a kip under a mangrove tree.) TRUE/FALSE

THEY HANG DOWN... | LIKE GREEN SPEARS. | I JUST DON'T SEE... | THE POINT OF IT - UGH!

**Answers:**

**1** TRUE. It splatters slimy juice and seeds everywhere. Guaranteed to liven up any school dinner.

**2** TRUE. Then the seeds germinate and the elephant is left hopping mad.

**3** TRUE. Beetles break into the pods and seed capsules and guzzle the seeds. If an elephant eats the pods the seeds survive but the beetles get digested.

**4** FALSE.

**5** TRUE. Australian mistletoe is a plant that grows on trees. It makes very sticky berries. The mistletoe bird eats the berries and gets rid of the seeds in their poo. But the seeds are also sticky – and they get glued to the bird's bum. So the bird wipes its bum on a tree (no – they don't use toilet paper). The seed sticks to the tree and that's just where the seedling wants to grow. You might like to explain these disgusting details when someone you don't like wants to kiss you under the mistletoe at Christmas.

**6** FALSE. The name comes from the popping noise made by the seed cases as they dry up and pop open to scatter the seeds. Which is odd because the sound is like pistol shots and often scares travellers. And it's nothing like a dinner bell.

**7** TRUE. Mangrove trees grow on muddy shorelines. The seeds are joined to green spikes and germinate on the tree. Then the spikes fall into the mud below. Roots quickly anchor the spike in the mud and a new tree starts to grow. If the tide is in, the spike floats away like a little boat for an exciting ocean cruise – in search of a new place to grow.

*Bet you never knew!*

*Orchids make tons of seeds. The European spotted orchid, for example, produces 186,000 seeds from a single plant. Naturalist Charles Darwin worked out that if all these seeds germinated, within three generations orchids would cover the Earth.*

*But most plant seeds fall in the wrong places or get eaten by birds or bugs.*

*This old rhyme says it all...*

Sow four grains in a row
One for the pigeon
One for the crow
One to rot and another to grow

Mind you, seeds are useful to people in unexpected ways...

## Better stick to the job

Swiss inventor George de Mestral had a problem. Ever since the zip on his wife's dress broke just as they were going out he'd been trying to invent a new kind of fastening.

WE'LL USE TAPE TILL I THINK OF SOMETHING BETTER

One day in 1950 George was out for a walk with his dog. He noticed the animal's ears were covered in seeds. They were burdock seeds. They stuck to the dog because they were covered with tiny hooks that clung to the animal's hair. This gave George the seeds of an idea.

YOU'RE A GENIUS, BONZO!

For the next eight years George worked out how to make a fastening based on the burdock. At last, with the help of industrialist Jakob Müller he made a breakthrough.

Together they came up with two strips of nylon. One

strip was coated with tiny hooks and the other with tiny loops. And the name of this new product was Velcro. Today it's used for fastenings on spacesuits and you might even have some on your clothes.

## Frightfully fruitful fruits

People tend to muddle up fruit and veg. Some think all fruit is sweet and veg isn't and that's the way you can tell the difference. But they're wrong. Not all fruits are sweet tasting. Some fruits taste savoury and some are disgustingly sour.

So let's ask a botanist to make things clear...

A FRUIT FORMS FROM THE SWOLLEN OVARY SURROUNDING THE SEEDS.

EH?

Well, the ovary was the bit in the flower that's at the base of the style – take a look at page 107 if you don't remember. After the flower is pollinated the seeds start to form and the ovary swells up around them. Make sense so far? So to be a proper fruit and not just a common or garden vegetable, whatever you're eating had to have started off as the ovary of a flower.

## Test your greengrocer*

* If you don't know any greengrocers you could ask your teacher instead.

Which of the following are fruits?

## Vicious veg expressions

Have all these scientists gone raving mad?

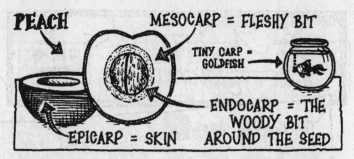

PEACH MESOCARP = FLESHY BIT
TINY CARP = GOLDFISH
ENDOCARP = THE WOODY BIT AROUND THE SEED
EPICARP = SKIN

Now, you might think that fruits are healthy and harmless. Tasty, even. Surely there's nothing vicious about a banana, is there? But believe it or not, people have fought and even died for fruits. Take the breadfruit for example. The what? No, I didn't make that up. Read on and discover the whole rotten story.

A breadfruit is a green fruit about 20-30 cm (8 inches) across. It has a bland rather boring taste but you can cook it in loads of interesting ways – roasting and frying and boiling it in lots of mouth-watering recipes. And best of all, it's cheap and easy to grow.

Too easy. In the eighteenth century the West Indies was full of slaves who were cruelly forced to grow sugar and tobacco for their wealthy masters. And the masters hatched a vicious plan to save money by feeding their slaves on cheap breadfruit. But first they had to get some plants from Tahiti where they grow.

The slave masters asked for help from Sir Joseph Banks (1744-1820), the boss of Britain's Kew Gardens. Sir Joseph asked the government to provide a ship, HMS *Bounty*, and hired William Bligh (1754-1817) as its captain. Then he hired a young botanist called David Nelson to collect the breadfruit trees. Here's how David Nelson might have described the voyage in his letters to Sir Joseph Banks...

130

# A fruitless journey

The Bounty, off Tasmania, 20 August 1788

Dear Sir Joseph,

I hope this letter reaches you safely. The voyage has been BRILLIANT so far. Thank you for sending me and thank you for sending your gardener William Brown to help me. We get on really well. Today we both went ashore and found some new species of plants which I look forward to showing you on my return.

But I'm afraid things aren't going so well between Captain Bligh and his officers. They have spent the whole voyage so far squabbling and bickering. They argue over accounts, supplies - every tiny detail to do with the ship. I don't blame the captain for these rows. Sure Bligh's got a really bad temper and he sometimes yells and curses at his officers. But someone's got to be in command. Anyway, I'm sure everything will be fine when we get to Tahiti.

Yours faithfully
David Nelson

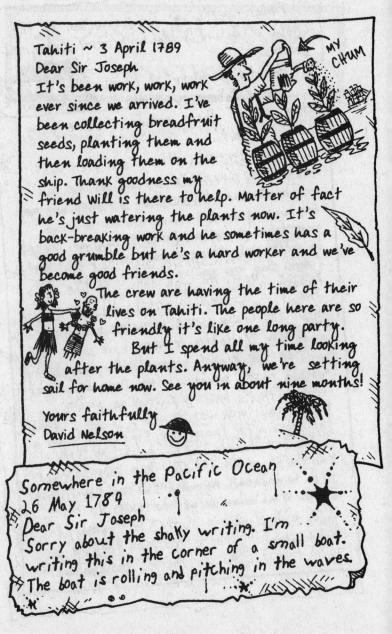

Tahiti ~ 3 April 1789

Dear Sir Joseph

It's been work, work, work ever since we arrived. I've been collecting breadfruit seeds, planting them and then loading them on the ship. Thank goodness my friend Will is there to help. Matter of fact he's just watering the plants now. It's back-breaking work and he sometimes has a good grumble but he's a hard worker and we've become good friends.

The crew are having the time of their lives on Tahiti. The people here are so friendly it's like one long party.

But I spend all my time looking after the plants. Anyway, we're setting sail for home now. See you in about nine months!

Yours faithfully
David Nelson

MY CHUM

Somewhere in the Pacific Ocean
26 May 1789

Dear Sir Joseph

Sorry about the shaky writing. I'm writing this in the corner of a small boat. The boat is rolling and pitching in the waves.

Four weeks ago I was woken at the crack of dawn by three grim-faced crew members.

"What's going on?" I cried.

"We're taking over the ship," one of them sneered. "We're going back to Tahiti."

"Yeah," agreed another, "and then we'll have some fun like we did before."

They were all laughing as they dragged me up on deck.

On the deck everything was in chaos. Captain Bligh was tied to the mast. He was shouting like crazy – he was so angry. And some of the crew were arguing and swearing. I saw William Brown.

"Help me, Will!" I cried. He just gave a nasty smile.

W.B.

And that's how I found out. Sir Joseph, I'm sorry to say your gardener, and my so-called friend, William Brown has joined the mutiny. How could he?

I said, "What about the breadfruit, Will?" He stuck his face up close to mine. "I'm sick of those plants," he hissed. "And the crew hate them too 'cos they've been going thirsty. All so there's enough water for your precious breadfruit. Well, now

133

we're going to chuck them all overboard."

All my lovely plants. What a waste of everything — I could have wept.

And that's how I came to be in this tiny boat. The rebel crew members forced me, the Captain and the Captain's friends into the boat and set us adrift. There are nineteen of us. We spend all day bailing water to stop the boat from sinking.

Food is running short. We share a morsel of bread each day. Oh, and there's a tiny slice of bread fruit for afters. I will try and write again. If I live.

Yours faithfully
David Nelson

Somewhere off the coast of Australia
4 June 1789
Dear Sir Joseph
I feel you or someone should know what has become of us. Of course, I know it's quite likely that this letter will never reach you. But I will write it anyway just in case.

We are still in the boat. And I feel sick and

very, very tired. At least my knowledge of plants has come in handy. When we land on deserted islands I search out the plants that are safe to eat. This makes a change from eating that disgusting breadfruit all the time. Then we set off again searching for a settlement with people who can help us.

I can't believe it - Captain Bligh is still quarrelling with the two officers who came with us in the boat. I blame the Captain for this mess. He just can't deal with people. We don't even have a map. All we've got is Captain Bligh's pocket compass. He says he knows which course to steer but the rest of us aren't so sure.

Bligh (the blighter)

I feel awful and fear I won't make it. I'm badly sunburned and I'm terribly weak. My feet and legs are all swollen from being cramped in this boat. Some times I feel like going to sleep and not waking up. Will we all die here in this boat?

I don't want to die.

David

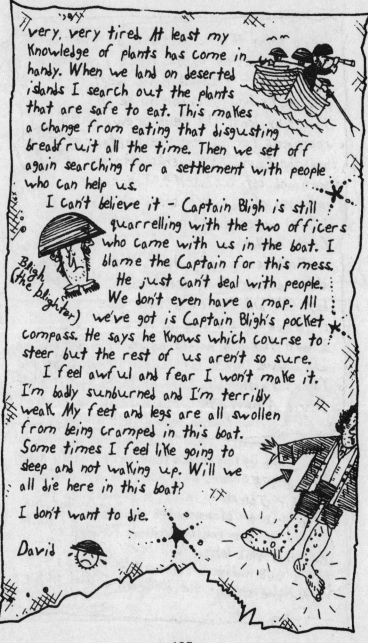

135

12 June 1789
Dear Sir Joseph

Things are getting worse. For ten days now we've had very little water to drink. Some of the men just lie in the boat staring at nothing. Too weak to move, I suppose. I've given up hope and have ceased to count the days. My body is covered in sores. This is the end.

Hold on. We've just sighted land! Yes – LAND! There are trees everywhere. We're not too sure where we are. I will write more when I have enough strength.

14 June 1789 ~ Coupang

We met a man in a fishing boat. He told us we were near a Dutch settlement! And we arrived this morning. Safe at last! And it's all thanks to Captain Bligh. He steered the course using just his pocket compass. What a wonderful man he is!

Bligh (my hero)

The Dutch people have been really kind. They gave us cakes and now I've got a nice comfy bed to sleep in. It's so amazing to sleep between clean white sheets. I feel a lot better. I'm really looking forward to going home at last.

Yours faithfully
David Nelson

HOME!

## A painful postscript

Don't read this bit unless you *like* unhappy endings. Sadly, David wasn't completely better. He went out looking for plants and caught a fever. He died a few days later. William Bligh said:

THE LOSS OF THIS HONEST MAN I VERY MUCH LAMENTED

In 1792 Bligh returned to Tahiti and fetched a new load of breadfruit. Although this time he reached the West Indies his mission was fruitless. The slaves didn't like the fruit and fed it to their pigs. It took years for breadfruit to become as popular a food in the West Indies as it still is in Tahiti today.

*Bet you never knew!*
*The soil is full of seeds. Lurking under every 0.84 square metre (1 square yard) of garden lawn there are around 30,000 seeds waiting to burst out of their capsules and grow into adult plants.*

*Now most seeds grow into weeds but some make useful plants that we can eat or make things from. They are the vital vegetables. Yes, it's time to get your teeth into those greens.*

EAT UP IF YOU WANT TO BE BIG AND STRONG LIKE YOUR FATHER

# VITAL VEG

We can't live without plants. Without plants there would be no oxygen for us to breathe and nothing to eat. If that wasn't bad enough, life would be much harder in loads of other unexpected ways because plants have strange and unusual uses. Yes, they're even more vital than you might think. And plants pop up all over the place...

Take school dinners for example.

**School dinner veg – the terrible truth**

You probably don't know it, but the vile vegetables served up in your school dinner have some interesting tales to tell.

**1 Odious onions**

SMELL GETS UP YOUR NOSE AND MAKES YOU CRY

BITTER TASTE

SMELLY BREATH

In the Middle Ages one writer on herbs claimed (wrongly) that eating onions was bad for you:

Onions make you cry because they contain a strong oil that turns to vapour when the onion is cut. This vapour makes your eyes smart. Does your school dinner move you to tears?

Onions are swollen leaf bases. The onion stores starch to help it grow the following year. In fact, lots of vegetables do this. Examples on your dinner plate include carrots, potatoes and parsnips. Of course, humans regularly spoil the plants' plans by gobbling them up.

## 2 Crunchy carrots

Originally, carrots were white or purple. That's the colour of wild carrots. The only wild orange carrots grow in Afghanistan and they were the ancestors of the carrots in your school dinner. Scientists reckon the orange carrots were brought to Europe by traders some time before the twelfth century. From there settlers and explorers took them all over the world.

## 3 Chewy cabbage

Cabbage probably isn't your favourite veg, but we're lucky today 'cos it used to taste even worse! Wild cabbage is bitter and leathery and grows naturally in Europe. But modern cabbages have been bred to produce juicier and more tender leaves. (Unless they're school dinner cabbages, of course.)

## 5 Boring baked beans

Yes, baked beans start off as plants. Baked beans are made from American haricot beans, which are actually seeds. The sauce is made from three more plants: tomatoes, sugar from sugar-cane, and cornflour from ground-up maize. In 1997 scientists were planning to test new kinds of bean that don't make you fart. But so far we haven't heard anything of the results.

## 6 Revolting rhubarb

Fancy some rhubarb for pudding? Rhubarb grows well when there's lots of manure in the soil. That's why country people used to tip their chamber pots over their rhubarb plants. This *probably* doesn't happen to your school rhubarb. One species of rhubarb *not* usually used in school dinners has a strong laxative effect. That means it makes you poo – three spoonfuls will clean out your insides!

### Sinister salad bars

Out of about 380,000 plants around 80,000 are edible. Humans normally only eat about 3,000 plants. But nowadays people have a taste for unusual plants. They're even served in posh restaurants… are you ready to order?

# THE PECULIAR PLANT PANTRY

 **Starters**

## GRATED BETEL NUT MIXED WITH LIME

As chewed in many parts of East Asia.
Delicious flavour helps to wake you up.

### IMPORTANT NOTE TO PATRONS

Don't eat too many. Juice makes your breath stink, turns
your teeth black and stains your mouth dark red. You can
spit out your starter in the spittoons provided.

~

## DELICIOUS DANDELION AND THISTLE SALAD

A crunchy green salad of dew-fresh dandelion
leaves and boiled thistle shoots. (Don't worry
we've cut all the prickles off – hopefully.)

### IMPORTANT NOTE TO PATRONS

Don't eat too many dandelion leaves. They make you pee.
Which explains their charming old name of "wet-a-bed".

~

## FRESH STEAMING STINGING NETTLE SOUP

Made with real stinging nettles. Tasty tender
young nettle tops simmered with fried potato
and onion. Full of vitamins and flavour. It's cheap
so it won't sting your pocket either.

## Main course
# INUIT LICHEN LUNCH

Tender lichens served nice and warm. It's tender because it's half-digested and cut from a freshly-killed reindeer's stomach. This is a traditional delicacy enjoyed by the Inuit people.

### IMPORTANT NOTE TO PATRONS
Don't eat too much. It makes you constipated (unable to produce poo).

## Optional side dish
# LUXURIOUS LAVER

That's a type of British seaweed that's scraped off the rocks and boiled with a little vinegar (optional). Steaming hot and black and slimy – just make sure you clean your teeth afterwards!

## Pudding
# DELICIOUS DURIAN FRUIT SALAD

Orangutans love it. Freshly picked in the forests of Sumatra, Indonesia.

### IMPORTANT NOTE TO PATRONS
Don't be put off by the revolting smell of rotten fish and sewage. Durians are banned in some hotels and on planes because of their vile smell.

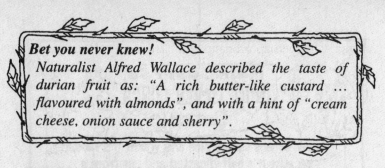

## Helpful and horrible herbs

What have vanilla ice-cream, ginger biscuits and pizza got in common? Yes, I know you'd love to guzzle them all. But they also all include herbs or spices that come from plants.

Ice-cream. Vanilla from a dried orchid fruit that grows in America.

Ginger biscuits. Ginger is the roots of a plant from South-East Asia.

Pizza. Chopped up oregano and basil leaves. Delicious!

Herbs are pleasant-smelling plants that you can use in cooking or use to make perfumes. Spices are strong-smelling plants used solely in cooking. Here are a few interesting specimens…

**1** Tarragon is a herb used to flavour tartar sauce, which is normally eaten with fish. The name means "little dragon" in Latin because people wrongly believed the herb was an antidote for snake bite.

**2** The herb saffron is used to flavour rice and give it an interesting yellow colour. It's made from the stigmas of a type of crocus. Saffron has always been expensive because in order to make 1 kg (2 lbs) of saffron you've got to pick up to 400,000 flowers.

In fifteenth-century Germany two merchants were burned to death for secretly mixing cheaper ingredients with the saffron they sold.

**3** Asafoetida (a-sa-fet-tida) is a spice made from the juice of a type of fennel plant from the Middle East. It stinks of rotten garlic but luckily when you cook it the smell disappears and all you're left with is a mild onion-like taste. So that's all right then.

## A moving story...

Humans have changed the plant world for ever. They've moved plants all over the planet to suit their ends. Just think of all that breadfruit sailing off to the West Indies. Many of the vegetables and fruit we eat originally came from many different places around the world.

Scientists reckon cherries first grew in Armenia and peaches first grew in China. Just go into any garden and you might spot fuchsias from South America, wisteria from China, azaleas from the Himalayas and tulips from North Africa.

But plants growing in a new country aren't always good news. Many rice fields in South East Asia are being taken over by South American water hyacinths that have escaped from gardens. Very pretty, but we can't eat it.

## Teacher's tea break teaser

Tap gently on the staffroom door. When it creaks open, smile sweetly and say:

But there's more to plants than food and drink. Some plants are special. They're so vital and useful that sometimes whole groups of people have centred their lifestyles around them. Take bamboo, for example. Just imagine you lived in the southern region of ancient China...

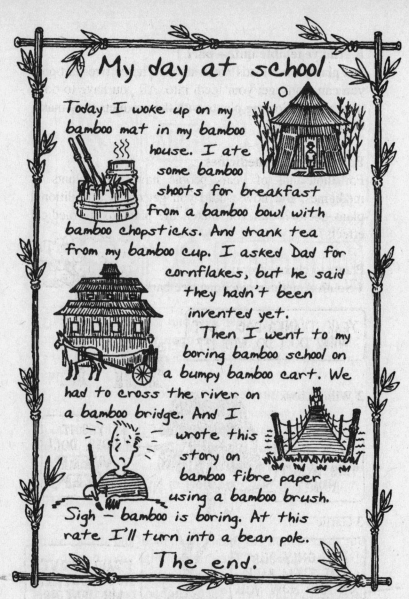

# My day at school

Today I woke up on my bamboo mat in my bamboo house. I ate some bamboo shoots for breakfast from a bamboo bowl with bamboo chopsticks. And drank tea from my bamboo cup. I asked Dad for cornflakes, but he said they hadn't been invented yet.

Then I went to my boring bamboo school on a bumpy bamboo cart. We had to cross the river on a bamboo bridge. And I wrote this story on bamboo fibre paper using a bamboo brush.

Sigh — bamboo is boring. At this rate I'll turn into a bean pole.

The end.

And if the teacher didn't like the story can you guess what his cane was made of?

## A vital vegetable quiz – part 1

But plants have loads more uses. Here's a two-part quiz you can really get your teeth into. All you have to do is match the following plants with the products they make. Go on – it's easy.

### Powerful plant medicines

For thousands of years people have used plants as medicines. But how would you get on as a traditional plant doctor? Can you match the plant to its medical effects?

Plants to choose from:
**1** South American cinchona tree bark

**2** Willow bark

**3** Garlic

YEAH, THANKS DOC – BUT WHAT DO I DO WITH IT?

KEEP STILL THIS WON'T HURT

YES IT DOES, DOC! **WEEP WEEP!**

I'VE ONLY JUST PUT THEM BACK ON AND NOW YOU WANT ME TO **EAT THEM**, DOC?

I SAID **CLOVES** NOT **CLOTHES**, MR JENKINS

**4** Castor oil plant

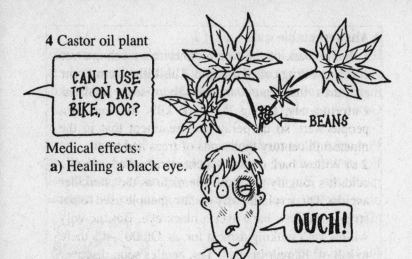

CAN I USE IT ON MY BIKE, DOC?

BEANS

Medical effects:

**a)** Healing a black eye.

OUCH!

**b)** Keeps your body healthy. Lowers your blood pressure, kills bacteria and speeds up healing.

YIPPEE!

**c)** A laxative that makes you go to the toilet and produce poo.

AT LAST!

**d)** Cures the killer disease malaria.

PHEW!

**Answers:**

**1 d)** The bark of the South American cinchona tree contains a drug called quinine. This kills microscopic creatures that cause the deadly disease malaria. Unfortunately, taking the bark kills the tree. But people were so desperate for treatment that in the nineteenth century thousands of trees had to die.

**2 a)** Willow bark contains a chemical called salicylic acid. It's roughly the same chemical as the painkiller aspirin. This explains why country people used to put strips of willow bark over a black eye. But the wily willow isn't making aspirin for us. Oh no – it's there to kill off hungry beetles. Yes, beetles soon discover that they're barking up the wrong tree. Ha ha.

**3 b)** Yep – these are official facts. Scientific tests have proved that chewing garlic is good for you. And as long as you've got your health, who needs friends?

**4 c)** Caster oil is a laxative. It was typically used to torture children. However, castor oil has a sinister secret. It has to be prepared carefully because the castor oil bean contains a poison so deadly that one bean can kill a person.

**Vital vegetable quiz – part 2**
**Priceless plant products**
Can you match the following plants with the products they make?
Plants to choose from:
1 Sugar cane
2 Stinging nettles
3 Seaweed
4 Wheat
5 Lichen
6 The South American bixa tree
7 Cotton
8 Rubber
9 Pine trees

Products to choose from:
a) A pair of very smelly socks
b) Fuel for cars

**c)** A nice plate of spaghetti
**d)** Dye
**e)** A dirty old wellie boot (where's the other one got to?)
**f)** Forecasting the weather
**g)** A tablecloth
**h)** Lovely orange hair
**i)** This book

**Answers:**

**1 b)** In Brazil sugar cane is made into alcohol and this is used as a fuel for cars. People buy it from pumps at garages alongside the more traditional petrol pumps.

**2 g)** In northern England, in the nineteenth century, people wove stinging nettle stems into tablecloths.

**3 f)** Laminaria (lam-in-ar-re-a) seaweed feels dry and brittle in dry weather but as rain draws near and the air grows moist, the seaweed takes in water and feels sticky.

**4 c)** Spaghetti is made out of pasta which is made from semolina. Yes, this is the same paste-like sludge that is served up as a school dinner pudding. And semolina is made from ground-up grains of wheat.

**5 d)** Lichens were used to make traditional dyes. A typical recipe involved leaving the dye to rot in a mix of stale pee and a chemical called slaked lime. Are you dying to make it?

**6 h)** Native South Americans use bixa seeds to make groovy orange hair colour. The juice also keeps mosquitoes away.

**7 a)** The cotton in your socks is made from hairs that help to disperse the seeds of the cotton plants that are inside their seed pods. The hairs are spun using machines to make the cloth.

**8 e)** Wellington boots are traditionally made from rubber. Rubber is made from the congealed juice, or latex, that oozes from the rubber tree when you cut its bark. Today a lot of rubber is made in factories using artificial chemicals.

**9 i)** Yes, you probably knew this one. This book is made from trees. That's where paper comes from. The wood is ground into a pulpy mass of tiny bits called fibres and dissolved using chemicals. Further chemical treatment follows including adding glue to stick the fibres together. This disgusting goo is then pressed and dried and cut to size.

THEY'VE GONE TO BE MADE INTO HORRIBLE SCIENCE BOOKS

### A tree-mendous discovery

The man who first thought of using wood for paper was French scientist René Réamur (1683-1757). One day René found an old wasps' nest in a forest. He took it home and found it was made of … paper. Further study proved that wasps chew up wood and sick it up to make this strange substance.

In 1719 Réamur excitedly told the French Academy that he had proved that paper can be made from plant fibres. (Everyone had forgotten that the Egyptians had been doing this with papyrus thousands of years before.) In Réamur's time, people used mashed-up rags. Although Réamur never made his own paper from wood, his work encouraged other scientists to make paper successfully from seaweed, cabbages, potatoes and old pine cones.

The first effective wood grinding machines for paper-making were developed in Germany in the 1840s.

So there you have it. Where would we be without plants? We eat them, we breathe their gases, and we take them as medicines when we feel sick. And we can make bridges and homes and run cars and make clothes and books and … well, everything.

# A blooming miracle

By now you may have realized that vegetables are vicious. Some of them guzzle insects even whilst the poor little creatures are still alive and wriggling. And vegetables are vicious to each other too – strangling their victims, sucking out their juices and stealing light. And that's just for starters…

But what do you expect? Just imagine vegetables were weedy little wallflowers that invited every peckish bug and munching mammal in for a free lunch. These nice scrumptious friendly little vegetables would stand less chance than a bag of chocs on a school bus. Everyone would want a bite. So vegetables have to be vicious just in order to stay alive.

It's a good thing too. Vegetables may be vicious but they're also vital for life. And that's more than you can say for humans. Well, just think about it … humans (and every animal) need plants in order to stay alive. But vegetables can do very nicely thank you without any of us.

And humans need *every* vegetable – not just the ones we eat or use to make things. Here's why. Every year botanists are finding amazing new plants that we can use for food and medicines. That means even a boring-looking weed could be tomorrow's wonder veg. It could even turn up in your local greengrocer's...

# The Wonder Veg Store
## just in. . .

### THE BRILLIANT BUFFALO GOURD
#### (Grows in Mexico and south-western USA)

▶ Huge 3-4 metre (9.8-13 foot) tubers.

▶ Weighs 30kg (66 lbs) when two years old.

▶ Very tasty and rich in vegetable oils.

▶ Feeds the entire family.

a lot DELIVERY EXTRA!

### THE WINGED BEAN
#### (it's a winged wonder)

A bean with wings. Don't like the sound of it? Don't scoff till you try it - you'll be eating your words. Yes, you really can eat the whole plant!

THIS PRODUCT IS REALLY TAKING OFF

▶ Leaves taste like spinach.

▶ Flowers can be fried.

▶ Seed pods taste like green beans.

▶ Seeds taste like peas.

▶ Tubers cook like potatoes (and they're equally good for you).

▶ All this and it makes the soil full of nitrates thanks to bacteria in its roots. Wow!

And on the medicine front scientists are looking at traditional vegetable cures used by native peoples. The aim is to make some of these remedies into drugs that can be used elsewhere in the world. For example, the cryptolepis (crip-toe-leep-is) plant of Ghana, Africa reduces fever and kills germs, but scientists have yet to find out which chemicals in the vegetable make it so effective.

And there's more to botany than finding new foods and drugs. Scientists have found out how to make entirely new kinds of vegetable. It's all done with genes, those little codes in the pollen and ovaries, remember? For example, scientists have taken a gene from bacteria that tells it to make a poison to kill caterpillars. The scientists added the gene to cotton plants. And now the cotton plants grow leaves that bump off caterpillars.

But the most amazing thing to do with vegetables isn't to do with scientists and their discoveries. It's to do with the vegetables themselves. It's the fact that vegetables aren't boring salad ingredients that sit around in gardens. They're incredible living beings. Even a boring little weed contains an awesome living chemical factory that can turn sunlight into food and make a cocktail of vicious poisons. It's enough to make a full-grown botanist weep with excitement and wonder.

OK, so vegetables are bit slow to get going. But who cares? Once you get to know their secrets vegetables are horribly brilliant.

And there's no doubt about it...

GREENS ARE GOOD FOR YOU!

And that's the HORRIBLE truth!

# HORRIBLE SCIENCE

**Science with the squishy bits left in!**